Rambam's Ladder

Praise for Julie Salamon's Previous Books

FACING THE WIND

"*Facing the Wind* is important not only for its lessons on the ravages of mental illness but for its ability to overturn our assumptions about evil, innocence, guilt, and compassion." — *The Wall Street Journal*

"*Facing the Wind* raises profound questions: of guilt, retribution, justice, redemption, and absolution. There are no easy answers. It is not a book that can be read and forgotten." — *The New York Times*

THE CHRISTMAS TREE

"With *The Christmas Tree* Salamon has confected a rich, heartrending tale…I can imagine Dickens himself sniffling and smiling." — *Newsday*

THE DEVIL'S CANDY

"Superbly reported…As close to a definitive portrait of the madness of big-time movie-making as we're likely to get." — *Newsweek*

"Salamon is the perfect reporter…She has the novelist's gift." — *Vogue*

"What makes *The Devil's Candy* valuable is not the author's insightful, objective reporting (it is that), but the sympathy she conveys in telling us what it meant to the people who were part of it." — *The New York Times*

THE NET OF DREAMS

"This moving, intimate, and often funny memoir demonstrates how the stories we must make up to survive can bring us to the actual truth after all." — *Salon*

Rambam's Ladder

It Is Necessary To Give
It Is More Necessary
To Know How

JULIE SALAMON

WORKMAN PUBLISHING • NEW YORK

Copyright © 2003 by Julie Salamon

CIP TK

ISBN 0-7611-2809-3

Permission TK

Workman books are available at special discounts when purchased in bulk for premiums and sales promotions as well as for fund-raising or educational use. Special editions or book excerpts can also be created to specification. For details, contact the Special Sales Director at the address below.

Design by Janet Vicario

WORKMAN PUBLISHING COMPANY, INC.
708 Broadway
New York, New York 10003-9555

Printed in the U.S.A.
First printing September 2003

10 9 8 7 6 5 4 3 2 1

To the men and women
of the
Bowery Residents' Committee

ACKNOWLEDGMENTS

I had a great deal of help as I tried to distill this huge subject into a short book. Perhaps the biggest stroke of luck was meeting the brilliant Natasha Randall, who became my matchless research assistant and invaluable sounding board.

So many people were generous with their time, their insights, and their stories. Deepest thanks to everyone whose commentary and experiences appear in the book. There were many others who provided crucial direction as well, and I would like to express special appreciation to: Rabbi Ayelet Cohen, Noelle Hannon, Maren Imhoff, Peter Johnson, Sharon King, Rabbi Sharon Kleinbaum, Rabbi Chava Koster, Laura Landro, Linda Levi, Mary Lindsay, Joan Malin, Muzzy Rosenblatt, Richard Salomon, Richard Shulman, David Tobis.

Thanks to friends and colleagues who indulged my passion for the subject and offered various kinds of inspiration, especially: Megan Barnett, David Blum, Bobby Cohen, George Colt, John Darnton, Madeline DeLone, Baby Jane Dexter, Steven Erlanger, Anne Fadiman, Monica Gregory, Trish Hall, Richard Heffner, Barry Kramer, Sara Krulwich, Wendy Miller, Lynn Paltrow, Andrew Tatarsky, Veronica Windholz. I am continually guided by the memories of my dear friend Conny Jean Frisch and my cousin Jeffrey Salaway.

I've learned that institutions can inspire a philosophy of giving, too, and I have been grateful for my family's association with Public School 3, the New York City Lab School; Greenwich House Music School; and the Village Temple, and send special thanks to Cantor Chere Campbell and Anita Hollander.

As always, I was kept on course by the advice—always sound and always cheerful—of the incomparable Kathy Robbins and her delightful team, with particular gratitude to David Halpern and Sandy Bontemps.

I have always known what generous souls are made of, thanks to my family. My late father, Alexander Salamon, and my mother and stepfather, Lilly and Arthur Salcman, have shown me firsthand that suffering can be transformed into empathy and enthusiasm for life. My sister, Suzanne Salamon, and her husband, Alan Einhorn, have reinforced those values in the next generation. As for my own little brood, Roxie and Eli, and my husband, Bill Abrams, their sweet, open hearts remind me every day where life's meaning lies.

Finally, ongoing thanks to Susan Bolotin, and to everyone at Workman who helped produce this book. Suzie asked me if I'd like to pursue this subject, and then brought her vast resources of wisdom, wit, and fine common sense to the editorial process. She has been a wonderful companion on this journey.

Contents

The Ladder of Giving

8

At the top of the ladder is the gift of self-reliance.
To hand someone a gift or a loan, or to enter into
a partnership with him, or to find work for him,
so that he will never have to beg again.

7

To give to someone you don't know,
and to do so anonymously.

6

To give to someone you know, but who doesn't
know from whom he is receiving help.

5

To give to an unknown person who knows you.

4

To hand money to the poor before being asked,
but risk making the recipient feel shame.

3

To hand money to the poor after being asked.

2

To give less to the poor than is proper,
but to do so cheerfully.

1

To give begrudgingly.

INTRODUCTION

We spend a lot of time thinking about why people are bad. Just as perplexing, maybe more perplexing, is why they are good. There are some obvious reasons: guilt, remorse, genetic predisposition, familial example, religious instruction, fear of social disapproval or, at the extreme, the terrifying thought of eternal damnation. But why for some people does it take a cataclysm to set off a charitable response, and why do others automatically reach into their pockets when they see a homeless person approaching? What kind of giving satisfies the need of a particular giver and where does that need come from? What are the rules?

I once believed it was natural to give. I grew up in one of the poorest counties in Ohio, in a rural town in Appalachia where my father was the only doctor. As far as I know, he never refused a patient for lack of money, and could enumerate whole categories of other people who weren't permitted to pay, including teachers and preachers. I would describe my mother as generous but pragmatic. She likes her giving to be balanced by a tax deduction. My own urge to give has many layers, built on a solid core of contrition. I've felt the need to

1

compensate for being raised without financial stress in a poor community, and for being the daughter of Holocaust survivors who had almost everything taken away from them but made sure I wanted for nothing.

So I've been volunteering at one thing or another most of my life, beginning as a candy-striper in junior high school. I didn't think about the why's too much, being absorbed with my family and work, but I confess to having felt slightly superior to people who were stingy with their money or their time. That cocky self-assurance about my own generosity was probably destined for some sort of comeuppance. I didn't expect, however, that this supposition about who I was—along with so much else—would be tested with a mighty life-altering blow. But that's what happened when terrorists attacked the World Trade Center, about a mile from my home.

On September 11, 2001, I felt no urge to give blood, make sandwiches, or search for the missing. My pervasive, all-consuming desire wasn't altruistic but maternal—to gather my children close and somehow protect them. There wasn't anything wrong with this impulse to protect my own, yet I felt selfish.

Maybe this was because my husband took action—or at least tried to. He went to offer blood and was asked to come back later; there were too many volunteers. He showed up at the cavernous Javits Center on a bleak rainy day to sign up for the rescue effort, only to realize with grim frustration, as he faced the long line of muscular working men, that his desk job had ill-prepared him for the tasks at hand. He picked up the flyer from a restaurant throwing a fund-raiser for the victims, down the block from where we live, and then made sure we gave a check, though we didn't attend the dinner.

Later, struggling to regain my footing, I recalled a story my mother once told me. World War II had just ended. She was twenty-two and living in Prague, having spent the previous year in Auschwitz and a work camp. Because she spoke several languages and was a hustler, she got a job with a charity that distributed clothing sent from America for the refugees, mainly Jews liberated from the camps. Among the perks: She was given an apartment, which she immediately crammed full of relatives and friends. And first crack at the clothes. In short order she refashioned herself from scraggly waif to chic young woman.

My mother's job required her to visit the refugee camps to find out what was needed. On her first outing, as she looked at the people she was supposed to help, she was overcome with uncharitable thoughts—disgust, actually. Her "clients" were dirty, still in rags, emaciated. She wanted to get away from them as quickly as possible. Later she felt shame, realizing her disgust mirrored the disgust the Nazi guards must have felt for her at Auschwitz. Then it was she who was dirty, ragged, pathetic.

All families have their stories, and in my family they became parables—in this case, a way of urging my sister and me to look carefully at people before we judged them as deserving of our praise or condemnation or pity. I always admired my parents for their belief in universal humanity, even after they had experienced evil so directly. Growing up with them, I learned firsthand the essence of charity.

How wonderful it sounds, so straightforward and pure. But even before September 11, holding on to those high-minded ideals had never been easy, not with so many charlatans and fanatics warping the benign view. After September 11, while I was glad others were searching for terrorists, for me the quest for goodness became far more compelling and urgent. I wanted proof that Stephen Jay Gould, the late paleontologist and essayist, had been right when he eloquently responded to the World Trade Center attacks.

"The tragedy of human history lies in the enormous potential for destruction in rare acts of evil, not in the high frequency of evil people," wrote Gould. "Complex systems can only be built step by step, whereas destruction requires but an instant. Thus, in what I like to call the Great Asymmetry, every spectacular incident of evil will be balanced by 10,000 acts of kindness, too often unnoted and invisible as the 'ordinary' efforts of a vast majority."

I began talking to people who were seriously engaged in

4

charity and philanthropy—high and low, givers and receivers—finding them via the principle of six degrees of separation. Over time, the ripple effect washed up a tremendous variety of insights, some provided to me by the very rich, some by the very poor. I also relied for sources and wisdom on the staff, board, and clients of the Bowery Residents' Committee, an organization helping the homeless of New York City. I have been involved with the BRC for years.

My touchstone, however, turned out to be someone distant from my time and place—a twelfth-century physician, philosopher, and scholar, who spent much of his life trying to reconcile faith and reason. He was Moses ben Maimon, known by the Greeks as Maimonides, and by many as Rambam, an acronym derived from the first letters of his name. Among his most significant works was a treatise on God and metaphysics—in the marvelously titled The Guide of the Perplexed—but his contemporary fame stems primarily from a hierarchy of giving he formulated. It is known as the Ladder of Charity.

What I first liked about Maimonides, especially as the absolutes of my childhood grew murky, was that he offered assurance that reasonableness is always complex. As I read him more, I found myself identifying with him, unreasonable as that might sound.

How could I not be drawn to someone whose writing and personal narrative resonate with startling relevance and universality? He lived through terrible disruption and exile, and yet carried on, not just to live his life but also to produce philosophical works brimming with humanity and hope. His pursuit of fairness was as dogged as his desire to transcend his own traumatic experiences and to encourage people to find their better selves. What an important message for today, particularly when we remember that he lived in a time when there had been significant philosophical, scientific, and cultural exchange among Jews, Christians, and Muslims.

Born in Cordoba, Spain, in 1135, during an era of peaceful coexistence among these three major religions, Moses Ben Maimon and his family fled when Islamic fundamentalists from Morocco invaded Spain in 1147. He wasn't even thirteen. After years on the road, stopping in Palestine for a time, then in Morocco, his family ultimately settled in Old Cairo. Maimonides thrived in Egypt. He became physician to the sultan, a leader in his own community, and a significant interpreter of Aristotle's philosophy. His prodigious outpouring of commentary on Jewish law—much of it written in Arabic—remains crucial to modern interpretation of ancient texts.

But make no mistake. Though much of his writing can seem arcane, Maimonides understood how to sell an idea. And perhaps no single idea was more important to his obsessive pursuit of righteousness than considering how to give with compassion and common sense. Tucked into ninety-three pages of exposition on proper treatment of the poor, he provided a handy eight-step program for giving. I think of it as Rambam's Ladder, preferring his almost rock-star nickname to the serious-sounding Maimonides. The more musical Rambam brings him home.

Rambam's Ladder is laid out in rungs of descending order, from the most worthy on down. The anonymous giver ranks above the giver who is known. Giving before being asked ranks above giving when asked. The lowest level belongs to the grudging giver; the summit belongs to the person who helps a poor man become self-sufficient. It is not a ladder to heaven—not for Jews, at least, whose good deeds guarantee no rewards in the afterlife. Indeed Maimonides starts at the top—the highest level of giving—and works his way down, moving from idealism to realism. In this inquiry, reflecting my desire for self-improvement, I suppose, I chose to climb up the ladder, ending with the most exemplary form of giving. But whichever way you look at it, the ladder provides an easy visual metaphor, a way to grasp the idea that there is giving . . . and then there is giving.

Maimonides didn't expect his eight-step program to answer every question. Witness the volumes of additional explanation he provided: an avalanche of elaboration and distinction, much of it specific to the agrarian medieval culture in which he lived. Almost everything has changed since then, but the desire to be good has survived, and so has the need to believe that we are righteous, even if not many people easily use that word today outside a religious context. Although private charity is knotted to public policy in uncomfortable ways, and the sheer mass of solicitations threatens to overwhelm individual good will, we still give, or think about giving, or plan to think about it.

For many people, however, charity poses no soul-searching for a simple reason: They feel it has little to do with them. Paolo Alavian fell into this category.

Born in Iran, raised in Italy, Alavian had emigrated to the United States to study pharmacy, but upon graduation decided to go into the restaurant business. He started as a dishwasher and twenty-three years later, at the age of forty-three, owned four restaurants in prime Manhattan locations. As a self-made man he was suspicious of people who put their hands out for money. There were exceptions. He almost always helped out (if asked) at fund-raising time for local schools. Not with cash—never cash—but with food. The gifts weren't perfunctory but nice meals, dinners for two valued at $75 or $100, attractive prizes for auctions.

Slender and intense with large sad eyes, Alavian believed in hard work and education. He would accommodate employees who asked if they could work dinners and not lunch because they were going to school—but in his cautious generosity required a letter from the admissions office every semester. Only once in his life had he made a cash donation to charity. He had vowed that if he ever managed to own a restaurant he would give \$500—a week's salary at the time of the pledge—to an organization that helped children. He kept his promise, and then never gave again. His excuse was that he had heard too many stories about charities that cheated, but in truth he didn't see why he should give. He was no Rockefeller. He was an immigrant who had become something from nothing.

The homeless people who wandered by the restaurant irritated him. That was the beauty of America, he felt, the sense of possibility that he'd never felt in other countries he had lived in—Iran, Italy, Austria. The homeless people hadn't taken advantage of opportunity, he felt. They must be lazy.

In the context of today's world, Alavian was neither an exceptionally selfish man nor was he altruistic. He tried to be a fair employer, a decent businessman, a caring father and husband, an honest member of society. Religion wasn't a significant force in his life. His family was Muslim but hardly orthodox; his father, a banker, enjoyed his wine too much for that.

So Alavian wouldn't have anticipated his reaction to the events of September 11, 2001. That he, who had been so focused on building a life for his family, would mastermind a community event whose purpose was simply to help others. It wasn't a grand affair nor did it require deep self-sacrifice. But it would change his perception of himself, his place in the world, his responsibility to others. As he said afterward:

"I'm not Mother Teresa. I'm not equal to her liver for generosity. But I believe that if you give from your heart you will have it returned back."

The World Trade Center was less than a mile from the restaurant that housed his basement office. Alavian had arrived shortly after 8 a.m. He had dropped his eight-year-old son at school, and was anticipating that the beautiful weather would translate into a busy day. He could set up sidewalk tables. Just as he was starting his paperwork, his wife called, asking if Alavian could take their three-year-old daughter to nursery school.

He was telling his wife with annoyance, "No, I can't do it. I have lots of things to do," when she began screaming into her cell phone, "Look at this idiot airplane flying very low downtown."

"You're seeing a movie," he said impatiently. "They're always filming." He hung up the phone and went upstairs to open the doors for the staff. Through the large glass panes facing the street he saw a lady in a red tenement building leaning out her window. He couldn't hear her, but she appeared to be screaming and screaming, pointing her finger to the south.

Alavian went outside and looked where she was pointing. He remained there, transfixed, until the buildings collapsed and the smoke made it impossible to see anything. Later he would remember that morning as a terrible dream, murky in detail but vivid in atmosphere. The woman with her silent scream. The customer who worked downtown and showed up at the restaurant, covered in dust. "Paolo," he said. "you have no idea what's going on." Other people wearing the debris of destruction streaming uptown. Nightfall coming early, as the air turned smoky and foul. Worrying about the gases that might be released by burning plastic.

The next day Alavian helped his landlord, the dentist next door, distribute hygiene masks. The day after that, he printed flyers inviting relief workers to drop by for free food. But after two or three days his generosity felt wasteful; the outpouring of food in the city far exceeded the need.

Still, Alavian felt compelled to do something. He couldn't stop thinking about the victims—not so much the poor souls who were killed but those who were left behind. Their faces, as he imagined them, filled his brain. "The wife who cannot see the husband, the kids who have no idea why the father didn't come back, the mother who didn't come back. What will happen to them?" he thought.

One morning over coffee he said to his wife, "Why don't we make some charity?"

From that idea, more of a spontaneous eruption, a plan emerged. He would throw a charity dinner at his fanciest restaurant. "We cannot forget, but for one night we can say, 'Let's go back to normal life,'" he told her. He would donate the food and ask people to pay what they wanted; all proceeds to go to the Red Cross. Once again he printed flyers, and began passing them out in the neighborhood and sending them to regular customers. His banker agreed to match whatever Alavian raised.

Alavian had no idea whether anyone would come; he told the kitchen staff to prepare for 70 to 80 people. By the time lunch was over he told the staff to prepare for double shifts. By the time dinner was done, 416 people had eaten and donated $76,000.

Even though he told them they didn't have to do it, Alavian's staff worked without pay that day and told customers to give their tips to the Red Cross. A woman who he knew had little money ate a salad and then wrote a check for $400. The construction crew working next door came for lunch. They had been driving him crazy in the days before September 11. Alavian was embarrassed recalling how he had screamed at them and called the cops, claiming their noise had disturbed his business. But the construction boss didn't seem to remember, or chose to forget. He ate lunch with his men, gave his check, shook Alavian's hand and then hugged him.

Paolo Alavian's act of charity was part of an amazing, almost reflexive reaction to the World Trade Center attack. The successful invasion onto American soil and the hostility that begat the terrorism provoked outrage, soul-searching, despair, fear, and a host of other emotions, many of them ugly and vengeful. But September 11 would also be remembered in the annals of charity as an unprecedented moment of giving. The desire to help that day was urgent, automatic, as though the balance of good and evil had tilted so far to one side that there was an instantaneous impulse to right the ship. Contributions to major organizations for the relief and recovery effort were estimated at $1.88 billion, with $1.25 billion coming from individuals. With predictable American enthusiasm and excess, there was an overabundance of giving. The Red Cross turned away blood donors; as Alavian discovered, sandwiches for rescue workers went uneaten.

As months passed, however, the impulse to give receded. Within a year the nation's blood supply was dangerously low, especially in New York City. Newspapers began writing about "compassion fatigue." The money that had been collected by various relief agencies generated some nasty fights over who deserved how much. The economy stagnated and the stock market declined, reducing the amount of cash available for charity (and eligible for tax advantages). Giving was politicized, as people in the United States became suspicious that Islamic charities were financiers of terrorism. A wave of corporate scandals generated a renewed cynicism about philanthropy. How else to react to the stadium, the cultural institutions, and the hospitals throughout Houston that bear the name of the Enron Corporation, when it was revealed that this corporate largesse was built on corruption—and at the expense of thousands of people who lost their livelihoods?

We were back to business as usual. In the past, scandals at major charities like the United Way had periodically erupted to undermine faith in organized giving. In April, 2002, Alfred Taubman, former chairman of Sotheby's, was sentenced to jail for price-fixing. His lawyers introduced his lifetime of philanthropy as part of his defense. The judge wasn't impressed. "One cannot give to the poor and steal from the rich," he said succinctly, as he sentenced the seventy-eight-year-old Taubman to a year in prison and a $7 million fine

Yet for many people, including Paolo Alavian, the attack on New York proved to be an awakening, an opportunity to finally understand what it means to be part of a community. Alavian's father used to say that many drops can make an ocean, but the son hadn't grasped the significance until his charity dinner. "I don't think anybody came that day to enjoy my pasta or my fish," he said months later. "They came to participate. I put them together but I am nobody without them."

Even Alavian's feelings toward homeless people have changed, though he hasn't become, as he said, Mother Teresa. "For me the revolution has happened. Now I realize that not everyone can make it. Now I see he may be young and look like he could work, but when you get close you see he has many problems—drugs, alcohol, disease, or bad habits," he said.

But he still sets limits on his giving that conform to his

vision of what it means to do good. When homeless people come by his restaurant he will serve them a meal, anything they want. He won't give money. "I always wonder what he is going to do with that money," he told me. "Is he going to have a beer?"

Thus, Alavian encountered the charity conundrum. How much to give and to whom? With conditions or without? How do you know if you're being cheated? Do you give until it hurts or only so long as benevolence feels good?

These age-old questions feel more complex in a world where philanthropy has become a big business, often depersonalized, stripped of spiritual content and meaning. Executive directors of large nonprofit organizations earn salaries that put them in the highest tax brackets, in part because they have bottom-line accountability. Yet it is difficult to assess a bottom line that measures human betterment rather than profitability.

The foundation world itself has become huge. In 1975, 21,877 foundations, with assets of $30 billion, gave away $1.9 billion. By 2000, there were 56,582 foundations in the United States; they gave away $27.5 billion from assets of $486 billion. This vastness can make an individual feel very small. How can an ordinary person compete with the very rich? What does a gift of a dollar, or even $1,000, mean when compared with the Bill and Melinda Gates Foundation's pledge of $24 billion to improve health care for the world's poorest children?

Yet people continue to add their drops to the ocean; in 2001 individual giving in the United States reached almost $161 billion, dwarfing the $9 billion given by corporations. Our society may be more materialistic than ever, less bound by religious strictures, yet giving has become a measure of probity. The Wall Street Journal reported in January 2002, "The public says it wants information about a company's record on social and environmental responsibility to help decide which companies to buy from, invest in and work for. By the turn of the century [2000], 26% of U.S. employees worked for companies that participated in United Way Campaigns, averaging a $170 donation per employee per year."

And in classic American entrepreneurial style, celebrating volunteerism has become another form of commercial exploitation. A Lands' End catalog salutes children who have done good works, and promises to donate $5,000 to each of their causes. Is the worthiness lessened by the fact that these "Born Heroes" are also promotional ploys for Lands' End products, which occupy all but the first couple of pages of the catalog? And is there anything wrong with turning giving into part of the search for profit?

Maimonides didn't address these questions directly; he was concerned with the most essential giving relationship, between the haves and the have-nots. He surrounded the eight levels of giving with pages and pages of explication, which may or may not be specifically helpful in deciding which brother's keeper to be, or in understanding why some people give and some people don't. Yet Rambam's Ladder has a straightforward simplicity that is both elegant and deceptive. Then and now, one step leads ineluctably to another, on a journey that can and should be pleasurable. After all, giving something is better than giving nothing, so why not enjoy the climb? True, the lowest rung on the ladder belongs to the person who gives with a frown, but that leaves seven other levels of giving on which you could—and should—feel gratified, without becoming smug. Maimonides grasped the profound connection between obligation and fulfillment.

As Paolo Alavian discovered, and as I would come to understand, giving may begin as a way to make order out of chaos, and turn out to be a transformation.

To give begrudgingly.

I don't remember when I first noticed him, but it seems to me that he had been panhandling outside the corner grocery for at least a year. He appeared to be in his late thirties, but since he was one of those ageless souls I could have been off by a dozen years in either direction. He was a pleasant looking man, African American, medium height but thin—too thin. He had a sweet face and warm smile and favored brightly colored T-shirts. When I walked by he would say, "How are you doing, sister?" He would make his pitch, almost as an apologetic afterthought. Then he'd say, "Have a nice day," even though I had responded, also apologetically, not with money but with advice.

"Go to the Bowery Residents Committee," (the BRC) I would tell him. I had been a volunteer at the agency for a long time, and had become chairman of its board. I had never questioned the agency's disapproval of panhandling: "Giving money, food or blankets directly to the homeless," its brochures spell out, "encourages them to stay on the street and avoid confronting their needs in a more constructive manner."

In other words, the BRC's goal and essential philosophy

mirror Rambam's. Aim for that highest rung, where a person can become self-sufficient.

That was my rationale each time I said to the man on the corner, "You can get help there," and then handed him a card with the BRC's address and phone number on it.

Always polite, he would respond to my unsolicited advice in different ways. He would tell me he wasn't interested in going to a program—guessing correctly that the BRC staff would encourage him to go into detox. Sometimes he would nod and say, "Oh, yes, I'll do that," both of us knowing he was just trying to get me off his back. Each time, he would examine the card and put it in his pocket.

That was the extent of our relationship, if these exchanges could be called that, for several months. I felt a friendly surge of recognition when I saw him, and then my body would tighten, sending warning signals that I shouldn't be supporting his self-destructive habits. It was at those times that I would cross the street to avoid him.

Toward the end of a warm winter came one bitterly cold day. I was walking home and saw David—though I wouldn't learn his name for some months—shuffling toward me. The shuffle was new.

It had taken me a minute to recognize him. He was not in what I thought of as his usual place, but out of context, a few blocks from his post by our corner store. I stopped and asked him what was wrong with his leg. He told me he had taken a fall. He looked miserable, although, as usual, he was neatly dressed.

My earlier reservations about helping him vanished. I asked him if he had had anything to eat yet that day. It was close to 1 P.M. He said no. I told him to come with me to the grocery store, where they also made sandwiches, and I would get him some food.

David looked surprised—he hadn't hit me up for money—but adapted deftly to this happy change in circumstance. He limped and I walked slowly up the street, past stores where $400 shoes are readily available; likewise $200 jeans, preripped. He told me, unsolicited, that he had stopped drinking. Did you go into a program? I asked him. He waved his hand dismissively. "I don't like programs," he said. "My body told me it was time when I woke up throwing up or everything I had tasted like beer. It's been a month since I had a drink."

I asked him where he slept and he said sometimes in shelters, sometimes in his "lady girlfriend's" apartment in Brooklyn, and often outside. He spoke with some poetry about the pleasures of sleeping outdoors on warm nights up in the Bronx, where he was from, and about how he enjoyed looking at the stars. I considered the possibility that I was being hustled, and suspected—no, knew—that there were grim stories being withheld. But he seemed happy talking about the stars in the Bronx.

Inside the store, the woman behind the register looked

disapproving, or so I imagined. Back at the deli counter, David ordered a hearty lunch: a sandwich with meat and cheese, some milk, a banana, some cookies, and chips. The bill came to $6.50.

"That's a good deal," David observed.

He thanked me and then we shook hands and went our separate ways.

I washed my hands when I got home.

I continued to see him on an irregular basis. He thanked me a few times more for the sandwich and then I found myself crossing the street again to avoid the old dilemma of whether to give him money. After about a month of this, on another spirit-chilling day, I saw him standing at his usual corner. This time I crossed the street in his direction, pulled five dollars from my pocket and just handed the money to him. After that I routinely gave him money before he asked, breaking one set of rules but conforming to another. At the time, I didn't know that I had moved up a notch on the ladder, where you give the poor man less than what is proper, but with a smile. Seeing David, reaching into my pocket, handing him money made me feel good. But now another question was left begging: Who was giving to whom?

The issue of self-interest is always in play when one is thinking about charity. How many people volunteer to work at the local elementary school auction after their children have moved on to middle school?

Between 1997 and 1999, David Dunning, a professor of psychology at Cornell University, and Nicholas Epley, a graduate student, conducted what they called a "holier than thou experiment." The experiment was aimed at measuring how well people calibrate their individual moral compasses: Are they as generous as they believe themselves to be? And are they able to anticipate the generosity of others?

In one of their studies, Dunning and Epley gave students five dollars each to take part in a fictitious psychology experiment. But the real test was to see how much of the payment the undergraduates would be willing to donate to charity. Most of the students predicted they would give away half, or $2.50, but thought their peers would give only $1.80.

As it turned out, they significantly overestimated both their own generosity and the selfishness of the other students. When confronted with the actual prospect of digging into their pockets, the students donated an average of $1.53, far less than what they thought they themselves would give, but not much less than what others gave.

In another study, conducted in the weeks before Cornell's annual Daffodil Days' drive for the American Cancer Society, the researchers asked students if they planned to buy flowers for charity and what they thought others would do. More than 80 percent of the students said they expected to buy flowers, about two flowers each, but thought only 56 percent of their peers would participate.

Once again, the students overestimated their own generosity but were more accurate regarding others. Only 43 percent bought flowers.

"Most people are overly optimistic about themselves," Dunning said at the time. "Even when we know that other people will be selfish, we think we're special, that the rules don't apply to us."

The holier-than-thou experiment started with an observation. The observation, Professor Dunning told me, was this: "Average people tend to think that they are anything but average. That they are more ethical, more intelligent, more everything than other people—especially in the moral or altruistic domain."

The observation led the professor to another question, actually two: "Do people have a good sense of their own moral character or are they overly cynical of other people? Or are they right about others but have too rosy a view of themselves?"

Were the results, I wondered, the discrepancy between intention and action, simply a case of old-fashioned false piety? Did the students want to believe—and have others believe—that they were generous when in fact they were stingy?

Not necessarily, said the professor. "When we're thinking about a situation hypothetically we think about what we should want to do and believe that we will follow our intentions. But when we get close to the situation we realize the sacrifice or loss involved. This may not be a conscious realization but it can stop us," he said. "Self-sacrifice is so noble because it's so hard. It's psychologically hard."

With charitable thoughts, then, can come ambivalence. Recognizing this, Maimonides places the reluctant giver on the lowest rung: the person who gives with the hand but not the heart. People may want to think of themselves as good but then agonize over how much to give. Maybe they want to give but worry about what it will cost them, in cash, psychological, emotional and even physical expenditure. Popular American literature feeds the dilemma. In *Gone with the Wind,* Scarlett O'Hara's mother dies, having become ill tending to charity cases. In *Little Women,* it's naturally noble Beth who becomes the narrative's sacrificial lamb.

The Cornell students, so confident in their own generosity, drew back when confronted with the reality of sacrifice. In my dealings with David, the sacrifice in question was less obvious. The problem wasn't that I was unwilling to give, but that I didn't want to relinquish control of my gift. I wanted to make sure it was being used in the way I wanted it to be used—for food rather than, say, for beer. Also, I chose to connect with David because I liked his face; I haven't struck up a similar relationship with the wild-eyed, muttering fellow wrapped in rags who also appears regularly in my neighborhood. I'm not saying I give only when I like the circumstances. It's just easier to muster a smile.

Contrary to my childhood belief (or wish), giving is not necessarily natural. Or at least it's not a law of nature. But inertia is. Most people I know feel overwhelmed by the requirements, real and perceived, placed on them every day. Eventually we figure out a manageable orbit as we juggle the demands of children, parents, spouses, ambition, health, and, yes, the pursuit of pleasure. But even so, it makes sense that it is easier to give to those causes that also fulfill some other obligation. In giving, as with everything else these days, we like to multitask.

In this category fall the kinds of donations I make all the time: to cancer research via the bike-a-thon my brother-in-law sponsors, or to homebound elderly people, who are helped by the money I pay to hear a benefit cabaret concert. Does the fact that I am, in part, motivated toward generosity by my love for my brother-in-law—and music—lessen the value of my gifts?

In the abstract, these acts of charity may not qualify as "100 percent pure," but Maimonides would have understood. The ground beneath the ladder of charity is always shifting, which is why he provided voluminous rules and aids designed to make it easier to give with the heart, not just the hand. For example, although he expected people to tithe, he didn't expect them to sell their property in a slack real estate market to meet their charitable obligations. What a practical man he was! And what a sympathetic one, realizing that we all need help climbing from the lowest level of grumbling obligation to the next level—that place where compassion flows more freely, and the smile on our face is a recognition of the recipient's humanity.

Consider for a moment the stacks of solicitations that come into your mailbox every month, all trying to seduce you, to get you to overcome your reluctance about giving. When you sort through them, you make a series of decisions. Some envelopes go into the wastebasket. Those solicitations touched neither your heart, nor your sense of obligation. But how are we to decide about the others, since we are asked not only to help the poor, but to support medical research, ballet companies, education, our religious institutions, the environment, peace and war—and not just in our neighborhood or even our country, but in the far corners of the world?

And when we do write a check, what are we trying to accomplish? Are we trying to guide society? If so, how much control on the rudder does that $100 check win you? To alleviate guilt-well, *only* to alleviate guilt? To feel as though you have some stake in the collective unconscious? And in the end, does it matter? Do an individual's motives mean anything compared to getting the job done-whatever it is? Why did Maimonides care whether the gift was offered with a frown or a smile, so long as it was offered?

Charity doesn't have to be selfless to be worthwhile-taking tax deductions for charitable donations does not diminish their value-but neither can it be a cover for graft. When teachers at a suburban school in New City, New York, began offering grade incentives to encourage students to participate in clothing drives and other social action projects, parents objected. This seems right.

It also seems right to deny companies that use charity to atone for corporate sins—those exquisite art exhibits sponsored by cigarette and liquor money—a place on even the lowest rung of the ladder. In contrast, however, imagine how high up are those few companies that treat charity as a corporate agenda, not as a postscript: Newman's Own, the company started by Paul Newman and the author A. E. Hotchner to sell their salad dressings, gives away 100 percent of after-tax profits to charities benefiting affordable housing, the arts, education, and disaster relief. Ben & Jerry's Ice Cream, while no longer owned by Ben Cohen and Jerry Greenfield, still includes in its financial statements a social, as well as a fiscal, audit. Maimonides would, I believe, have approved. I also believe that he would have welcomed "strategic philanthropists," companies that tie their giving to their business objectives, to the community of reluctant givers. These days that would be a very large community indeed, since most businesses, in the name of corporate responsibility, now give money to get something back—improved image, political currency in the community, shareholder goodwill—or to cover the chairman's obligation to his cronies.

Yes, giving has become yet another marketing tool.

Charles Raymond, president of the Citigroup Foundation, oversees strategic philanthropy at Citigroup, the financial services concern that gave away $68 million in 2001, in more than 3,000 grants of varying amounts. This sounds like a lot of money until you consider Citigroup's earnings; $14.1 billion that year on revenues of $67.4 billion.

Raymond, a tall thin man, gray-haired yet boyish at sixty, treated me to lunch in the executive dining room at Citigroup's Park Avenue offices in New York City. The room was airy and sleek; the elegantly prepared food served on beautiful plates. There were plump fresh berries for dessert, plus a plateful of delicious cookies, crisp and buttery. As I ate, I thought about the deli sandwich I'd bought for David, and wondered how much this lunch cost.

Raymond, who makes decisions about how much Citicorp gives and where, was candid about the public relations aspect of corporate giving. "We are a target for everything and everybody," he said. "We have issues of human rights, labor issues, environmental issues, everything you can imagine. Because we're in so many countries we are cited as bad guys in all kinds of things. It's very tough to always walk the line between being environmentally sound and working with the inordinate number of countries we work in and governments we work for. You cannot have more than 100 million customers and not have people who are doing bad things. So we're always on the defensive. Our philanthropy very often is something that takes a little bit of the edge off."

Raymond is a decent man who manages to live the good life—home in an exclusive suburb of Connecticut, the corporate dining room, town cars to take him where he needs to go—while aiming to do good. He had once been New York City's commissioner for homeless services, then had been executive director of the New York City Ballet, and now sat on the Bowery Residents' Committee board with me. He has a sincere commitment to spreading the wealth, at least a little, and understands how self-interest can be used as a practical way to overcome reluctance—for people as well as corporations.

He realizes that institutions like Citigroup wouldn't be as inclined to give without laws like the Community Reinvestment Act, which requires banks to give something back. "The community says to us, 'What the hell are you doing for us?' We strategically target organizations we think are doing good work in the community but that we also think will give us some visibility." In other words, companies that might not immediately think about dipping into their pockets, no matter how deep, are "encouraged" to give.

In some ways Raymond sees the irony of his situation. One year he gave a large grant to China to plant trees and to set up management training programs—not because these were the worthiest causes, but because Citigroup was planning a major expansion in China. But he also realizes the power he has to effect some good—as he defines it—even if the motive is more capitalistic than spiritual, more hand than heart. He would argue that the two are not mutually exclusive, though not always easy to reconcile.

The challenge laid down by Maimonides, to hardwire giving into your soul, feels remote from this bureaucratic process ultimately designed to further the interests of Citigroup. Yet it is clear that Raymond's work is close to his heart, and that giving motivated by self-interest should not be instinctively dismissed as unworthy. Even the frowning giver, sourpuss that he is, grabs a toehold on Rambam's Ladder. Yet the fact that there are eight levels, not one, indicates that charity requires constant examination of motive.

That thought was echoed in an e-mail I received from Jerusalem, in response to my inquiry into charity. "It says in the Torah one should not avert your eyes to avoid seeing a needy man—don't pretend not to see him. Simple as that," wrote my mother's first cousin Jimmy Weiss.

My mother had suggested that I contact Jimmy. "He is a very smart man," she reminded me. "A learner, like his father." His father, my great-uncle Herman Weiss, worked as a grill chef by day and a scholar by night, studying philosophy and religion in Spanish, German, Yiddish, and Hungarian. Jimmy's mother, Margaret, was an inspiration to me, a professional woman—a pharmacist—who could also bake. Her specialty was a soothing dessert she called "carrots cake."

Jimmy had spent time as an actor before he became a teacher, and as a devout agnostic before he became an Orthodox Jew. Since his retirement, he'd been studying the Talmud and the stock market, the latter being the subject of his many e-mail communications with my mother.

"What do the teachings of *tzedakah* mean today, not only to Jews but to the world?" I asked him in an e-mail. *Tzedakah,* which has come to be thought of as the Hebrew word for charity, is derived from the Hebrew word *tzedek,* or justice, and means righteousness. "Moral high ground seems so illusory these days," I wrote. "I'm desperate to find some."

Cousin Jimmy wrote me a long and valuable response, including an insightful summary of Rambam's Ladder: "In Jewish law attitudes of the giver can be more important than the amount of money involved. You can kill the soul of a person by giving him an insincere smile while administering your bounty."

Reading that passage made me understand why I'd confine Citigroup's largesse to the bottom rung of the ladder. The progression Maimonides had in mind was something larger than transference of wealth, something more important than social engineering. He was aiming for something more ephemeral, nothing less than the achievement of a just world.

That may be a big thought to attach to the donation you make to a school fundraiser, particularly if it's a gift to the school *your* child attends. But in truth, these self-interested acts of charity can be very pure, since they often focus on the positive effect on the recipient rather than the inconvenience or sacrifice of giving.

Or, as Jimmy wrote in his e-mail: "The most powerful thing one can say about *tzedakah* is that the act binds one to the poor receiver in a remarkable transaction. If you think about it, the act of giving to someone in need, especially a total stranger, closes the space between you in an amazingly intimate way."

He then offered a story that began to show me how easy it could be, in some situations, to skip the first step, to forego reluctance, on the climb up Rambam's Ladder.

"Once on a Saturday night, when I was waiting at the 34th Street subway stop, I saw a man, totally inebriated, drunkenly lose his balance, fall off the platform, and land between the tracks in the path of the oncoming train, which could be heard bearing down in the distance. Somehow he survived the fall and sat bolt upright, exactly between the two rails. As I remember it, he crossed his arms on his chest and started to sing. Without thinking of the dangers involved, I threw away the newspaper I was holding, jumped down onto the subway tracks, pulled the man off the floor, and half threw him up to where others could grab him and hold onto him until I got to safety, too. I wondered how this thin man could weigh so much.

"My behavior immediately after the heroics seemed to

be very inconsistent and strange. I felt I needed to put my arm around the drunk and keep him from harming himself anew. I felt very strongly that I had to continue to protect this drunken man and shield him from others until I could sober him up and take him home.

"It was as if I'd become responsible for him because I had saved him; giving him another chance bonded me to him in unlikely ways. I thought I had acquired a new cousin or brother, and I clearly remember calculating how to include him as if he were a new member of my extended family.

"When the authorities arrived to take charge of the situation it took a lot of cajoling before I released him to the transit police. 'Is he your relative?' they asked. I remember saying quite clearheadedly, 'I think so, but I'll give him to you for now.'

"What I felt then I now experience when I give *tzedakah*. I bridged the gap between us and felt the impact of my responsibility, temporary though it was, for the drunken man's welfare. I had taken on *his* responsibility. So, as I felt the closeness and the whisky breath, I had learned the lesson of giving. I am changed to this day by that event and that moment of bonding."

Like the people who gave on September 11, or who jump into a swimming pool to save a drowning child, my cousin Jimmy discovered that a true emergency can eclipse self-interest. There's no time for reluctance or regret, for second thoughts or analysis. You just give.

Responsibility 8

Anonymity 7

Corruption 6

Boundaries 5

Shame 4

Solicitation 3

Proportion 2

Reluctance 1

To give give less to the poor than is proper, but to do so cheerfully.

W hat is the proper amount to give? A friend in Maine says his parsimonious father took a democratic approach: He responded to every charitable solicitation he received by mail with a $1 contribution—if the charity in question sent along a prepaid return envelope. Another friend, a wealthy man, gives no money to charity. He believes the considerable sum he pays in taxes covers his debt to society. Warren Buffett, one of the richest men in the world, has a different philosophy, which is that since he can make money better than everyone else, that's what he should do. He plans to give it away after he dies. In the United States, most people don't have the wherewithal to follow Buffett's example, but they do feel compelled to give. In 2000, 78 percent of adults said they had made a charitable gift, averaging about $886 per person. Individual giving in the United States was 1.8 percent of personal income in 2001, about the same as it had been for several years.

We are a nation of data-gatherers, compiling and measuring. But can you quantify righteousness? Maimonides implied that you could and should, otherwise why would he place second lowest on his hierarchy of giving the person who gives the poor man less than what is proper. And what did he mean by "proper"?

The biblical injunction is to tithe, to give 10 percent. Then the tax code came along to complicate matters. Do you calculate the tithe from gross or net, before or after taxes?. Do you subtract that portion of your tax money that goes to social services? There's no clear-cut answer, but some in the world of philanthropy have suggested that we should tithe on our *disposable* income (the money left over after essential expenses, including taxes) and savings. But surely this leaves room for interpretation: One man's essential spending is another's luxury.

This moral ambiguity existed long before the IRS; the tithe was always subject to interpretation—endless amounts of it. In his treatise "Gifts to the Poor," Maimonides spends pages and pages differentiating between crops subject to tithing and those that are not. Figs and vegetables are exempt because they aren't harvested all at once, while garlic and onions are included because they are brought in for storage.

The rules go on and on. You are commanded to clothe the poor man and buy him furniture. If he isn't married, you are supposed to help him find a wife. If the poor person is a woman, you are supposed to marry her off (this was written, remember, in the twelfth century). Charity begins to sound a lot like meddling.

This ever-expanding template for order bespeaks an overwhelming desire for fairness and good will. In Rambam's dizzying array of regulations and elaborations lies a sense of frustration, a desperate compulsion to set things right. His treatise on the poor feels like an act of reconciliation and a defiant denial of reality, given the life he led, described by one biographer as "trouble and tragedy." His mother died in childbirth when he was a year old; he spent much of his life in dangerous exile; his beloved brother died at sea, a hurt so profound Maimonides spent a year in bed. Again proving it isn't always easy to practice what you preach. "Avoid both hysterical gaiety and somber dejection, and instead be calmly joyful always, showing a cheerful countenance," he once advised.

Maimonides understood that quantifying morality might be impossible, which didn't stop him from trying, however. But he also realized that putting a number or percentage on giving provides the illusion of control. The tithe, or some other compulsory amount, can reduce the pressure by offering certainty. Yet there is no certainty. Like the boundaries of love and hate, charity's borders keep shifting; its purpose and meaning can be elusive. By the time Maimonides is finished offering instructions on how the poor should be treated, charity has gone well beyond the tithe to become an intrinsic part of life.

Which well may have been his point.

Every charitable act has its own equation, depending on the variants of each individual life. What is the order of responsibility, after family and friends are taken care of? Does my neighborhood homeless man take priority over the starving child in Somalia? Or is it women and children first, no matter where they are located—or has equality taken women out of that mix? How can you buy yet another computer game for your imploring seven-year-old when you know the equivalent amount could, in many countries, feed a family for a week? Is there an amount that will assuage the guilt? Who, exactly, are we supposed to help and how much are we supposed to give them—whoever *they* are?

In 1906, a contemporary of George Bernard Shaw, a fellow social critic named St. John Hankin, wrote a shrewd comedy called *The Charity that Began at Home,* about a family plagued by an excess of charitable desire and a shortage of common sense. Under the sway of on organization called "Church of Humanity," Lady Denison and her daughter are not only kind to orphans and sick people, but feel obliged to tolerate rude servants and vile houseguests. "You see," one character explains, "people don't need friends to be kind to them. They have plenty already. Disagreeable people have not."

"It's not what people deserve," he continues, "but what they want that matters, don't you think? In fact, often the less people deserve the more we ought to help them. They need it more.... Usen't we to be taught that it was our duty to love our enemies?"

"Yes," another character replies. "But only on Sundays. And no one ever dreamed of doing it."

Hankin's characters were products of late Victorian England, and beneficiaries of the enormous wealth British colonialism had brought home. Their circumstances contrasted sharply with the miserable living conditions not only in the countries that fed the Empire's appetites, but within England itself, where poverty was widespread. The British responded with charity, which in turn led to the development of the welfare state and modern philanthropy—and to a literary tradition of social criticism.

Today, as the most powerful nation in the world, the United States carries the burden of noblesse oblige—an uncomfortable position for a country that rejected the monarchy in favor of individual self-sufficiency and potential. Unlike England, which ultimately decided charity should be compulsory, taken care of almost entirely by the government, the United States—despite conservative complaints about the reach of the welfare state—still relies heavily on private giving. Religion captures the largest number of charitable dollars, but it has a lot of competition. Foundations have proliferated like kudzu in recent years, and they are dedicated to every cause imaginable. There are foundations to advise foundations, to build Web sites for them, to advise people on how to start them, and foundations to monitor how well foundations spend their money. Apparently they could spend it a lot better than they do: A McKinsey and Company report estimated that charities could free up $100 billion a year by changing their fund-raising techniques and improving sloppy management habits.

At the beginning of the twentieth century the sociologist Max Weber linked the rise of capitalism to the Protestant work ethic; today charity itself has become a noticeable factor in the U.S. economy. Near the end of the century, the United States had 1.2 million charitable, social-welfare and religious groups, employing 10.9 million paid workers and 5.8 million volunteers, accounting for an estimated 6.1 percent of the national income in 1998, or $443.6 billion.

Charity has become a profession, and yet it seems that materialism has trumped altruism. Most people agonize far more about acquiring than giving: Think of the amount of time you spend immersed in catalogs; compare that to the attention you pay to your charitable donations.

Political leaders exhort us to volunteer, to give to the needy. Yet the United States hasn't been able to secure a foothold on the second step of the ladder, which requires that giving should be proportionate to the suffering. We have more billionaires than any country in the world—216 out of 497 in 2001. Yet the U.S. Bureau of the Census reported in

September 2002 that 32.9 million Americans were officially considered poor, 9.2 percent of the total population.

If worldwide suffering is thrown into the equation, the imbalance becomes even starker. The United States, now the world's only superpower, does not equate military, economic, and cultural dominance with charitable duty overseas. Somehow it's always easier to finance bombing than building—or rebuilding. In 1992, the twenty-two richest members of the Organization of Economic Cooperation and Development agreed that they should target 0.7% of gross domestic product for overseas aid. By the turn of the century, almost all the rich nations had consistently failed to reach that goal— the smallest contributor by percentage although largest in dollar amount, was the United States, the world's richest nation. And, just as Citigroup links its charity to business opportunity, so the United States ties charitable giving to military and economic objectives and complains when our philanthropy does not achieve the desired results. J. Brian Atwood, former head of the United States Agency for International Development (USAID), said in a speech to the Overseas Development Council. "Despite many well-publicized trade missions, we saw virtually no increase of trade with the poorest nations. These nations could not engage in trade because they could not afford to buy anything."

No wonder people become cynical about charity. It's so easy to dismiss it as corrupt or ineffectual or a tax dodge, to disdain the pieties and self-congratulations that can be associated with giving. And it's often easy to find your beneficence tested by ungrateful recipients. But isn't it also possible to see charity as a transaction in which the terms are constantly being reevaluated, understanding that the view changes as you climb the ladder?

Talking to all kinds of people involved with charity, I found almost no one who was concerned with fixing a percentage for giving. Like Maimonides, they were interested in something more profound than rote donation. They wanted to find a different kind of formula, an equation that uses charity as a bond between people.

"My view is that too much emphasis is put on dollars or cents or shekels or lire in this whole discussion," said Vincent McGee impatiently when I asked him if it was possible to find a mathematical solution. McGee once thought he would become a priest—and attended seminary—but ended up advising rich people on how to give away their money. When I met him, McGee had just spent eighteen years helping his largest client, Irene Diamond, the wealthy widow of a New York real estate developer, disperse a large percentage of her husband's fortune.

"I'm always very nervous about code words or buzz words or labels," he told me. "Don't talk about charity or philanthropy, but talk instead about involvement. Communities have extraordinary resources and part of the challenge is to figure out how to make those resources effective to the individual, their immediate family, the community as a whole. Not to think of it as giving but as basic participation. It may be just a meal or a ride to the grocery store for a shut-in. It may mean $10 or $100, or active involvement in the PTA to get a crossing guard, and maybe that will escalate to participation in the political process. To me that's what being a human being really means."

Webster's *New World College Dictionary* distinguishes between charity and philanthropy. Charity, by the first definition, is "the love of God for humanity, or a love of one's fellow human beings." Philanthropy is "a desire to help mankind, especially as shown by gifts to charitable or humanitarian institutions." Oversimplifying, you could say that charity addresses an immediate need and philanthropy addresses the problem that causes the need. Giving either way conforms to McGee's philosophy.

McGee operates in rarefied circles; his other clients have included Swannee Hunt, a member of the Dallas oil family and former ambassador to Austria, and her sister Helen. But his own background was New York working class: his father was a laundry deliveryman for the department of sanitation and his mother was secretary to the local Catholic parish. McGee was the child designated to become a priest, but after eighteen months in Catholic seminary he decided he wanted a broader experience.

He got that. During the Vietnam War he became active in the antiwar movement, a calling that paved the way for his career—and also put him in jail for a year, as a draft resister. Before going to jail, however, he ran an organization formed by a group of 6,000 business executives opposed to the war, and learned how to broker deals in which the endgame wasn't profit but fulfillment of a purpose.

McGee believes proportion is a moral rather than a mathematical question. For him, the appropriate measure is action, and he can tell you exactly when he came to this realization. It was 1966 while he was still in college. He read an article by Paul Goodman, "The Psychology of Being Powerless," in *The New York Review of Books*. The gist of which he recalls like this: "The moment a person decides they can't do something about an issue or a decision, they make themselves powerless and give their power to someone else who might not use it so objectively or altruistically." For McGee, charity should be seen as power, a catalyst for political action and the development of the soul, but you have to do the measuring yourself.

A pound of pennies doesn't equal a pound of $100,000 certificates of deposit, but the amount of money someone gives can be misleading, says Michael Margitich, deputy director of development at New York City's Museum of Modern Art (MOMA). "We can get a letter from a $25 donor that's just as impassioned as that from any other donor," he told me. "There's definitely a sense of ownership, the sense that this is my museum, my orchestra, my ballet group."

Margitich acknowledged that giving to the arts isn't the same as charity, because the reciprocity—the desire to be exposed to paintings, music, dance—is more evident and explicit. But many of the same principles apply, and so do many of the questions. While an institution like MOMA can't survive without its heavy hitters, Margitich believes that passion is a crucial component that must be included in any assessment of proportion. He understands this best from his experience as a donor, not as a professional fundraiser. He began giving to a guide dog foundation in upstate New York because he admired their marketing strategy: a little chart the organization sent him that explained exactly how many dogs can be trained for $100.

Passion came into play only after he sent in his $100 and received a personal card from the director of development. "I was so moved I sent another check in," he said. "That was so nice. Here I am, in the business, and that was my reaction. It touched me."

What is it worth to touch someone, or to be touched? And how to you measure the value of time, of love, of the simplest gesture that can alter the course of somebody's life? Can you apply accounting principles to righteousness?

In the 1990s, when WGBH, Boston's public television station, revived a twenty-year-old program called "Zoom," a children's variety show performed and conceived by kids, the producers decided to introduce segments on volunteerism, which hadn't been part of the show before. The program was inundated with videotapes showing children organizing penny drives for charity, having their hair cut at a salon that donates the cuttings to make wigs for kids with cancer, collecting money at a birthday party to buy dog food for the local animal shelter.

The idea began, explained Kate Taylor, director of children's programming at WGBH, because she and the show's consulting psychologists felt that children were looking for some spiritual connection. They'd already observed that children growing up in the 1990s had been indoctrinated with ecological awareness and were wondering if that sensitivity could be extended. The "Zoom" segments encouraged action over the simple donation of money. "We wanted situations where they actually make a connection with somebody and learn about mutual appreciation that comes with giving and receiving," said Taylor. She felt so strongly about this that, after September 11, she and her collaborators decided they should produce a segment focusing on community service. Taylor, who is also a mother, had a personal stake.

"For kids, who feel completely disempowered by the World Trade Center and their terrible vulnerability, with war in the world, it's important to feel they can make a difference, make their communities stronger. We did a segment about a group of kids who went to their local firehouse, not in New York, just to thank them for what they're doing. Volunteerism can be a way for kids to get through this period where there's nothing they can do. They can't vote. They have no say in how things are going to unfold, but what they can do is take some positive action so they don't feel like sitting ducks."

While understanding that "Zoom" can't possibly be a substitute for parental example, the WGBH producers wanted to instill in children the ethos of giving, to wire them so that they associated good deeds with a good feeling. Otherwise, Taylor said, they will grow up to be selfish givers, the volunteers who show up only when it's convenient, or who are so intent on fulfilling their personal goals that they lose sight of the essential purpose of charity: to help *others*.

Carmen Vega-Rivera is the executive director of New York City's East Harlem Tutorial Program, which provides volunteer tutors for high school students from the neighborhood, where the schools have poor track records. The students—about 400 every year—are Puerto Rican, Mexican, African-American, and a few Asians; the volunteers used to be all Caucasian until Vega-Rivera took over in 1988, and began encouraging people of color to volunteer. Now only 60 to70 percent of the tutors are white.

It's a big commitment—two-and-a-half hours a week for an entire school year—but most volunteers feel good about the connections they make, and the opportunities that the program opens for children who haven't had too many lucky breaks. But occasionally, Rivera said, the volunteers arrive with disproportionate expectations. "You'll get a volunteer who will say, 'I want to work with so and so in the sixth grade so she'll go to an Ivy League School.' We have to tell them not to impose their own values and expectations."

She told me about a volunteer who spent an enormous amount of money on clothes for a student who showed up wearing a sweater with holes. Again, a matter of proportion. In this case, less would have been more. But that was nothing compared with the volunteer who bought his student a car.

"What was that person thinking?" Vega-Rivera asked, laughing, her glasses slipping down her nose.

I understood her frustration, but I could also imagine what that volunteer might have been thinking, or wishing: that one lavish gift could just take care of *everything,* redress the imbalance with a Hollywood notion of a happy ending.

When Vega-Rivera told me this story, I again was reminded of how quixotic the pursuit of righteousness and justice can be, particularly when evil and inequity are so persistent.

When I had gotten off the subway at 103rd Street on the east side of New York, on my way to the interview, I'd felt as though I'd entered another country—one that was Spanish-speaking and poor—even though I was less than six miles from my home, land of the $400 shoes. I walked by a large public high school where a fire was burning in the concrete-paved yard; black smoke poured into the sky.

As I entered the bright blue tenement building that housed East Harlem Tutorial, a cheerful exclamation point in a drab landscape, my mind filled with gloomy thoughts. The Pentagon was warning of possible nuclear attacks and another war was on the horizon; the Israelis and Palestinians were murdering one another—again—at an alarming rate; the Roman Catholic Church was awash in scandal over priests molesting children. American corporations were more in the news for their corruption than their innovation. How would Maimonides feel about his quest in this world?

Some days the ladder feels very shaky. So I think about people like Carmen Vega-Rivera, people with a utopian sense of proportion, who decline to place a limit on their dreams. She affected me most with a story about why she does what she does.

"I was raised not far from the Bowery and we could walk there," she told me. "and I would see men suffering. I was born in 1954, so this was the '50s and '60s. I always sympathized with the men on the Bowery. Why were they in the situation that they were in? Why were they suffering?

"I remember having a discussion with a man, and learning that he was actually a professional who had hit rock bottom and had lost everything. That really took a toll on me. I would have these dreams that one day the tip of Manhattan would break off and that all this money would come from somewhere and we would help all the men of the Bowery get cleaned up, get their feet back on the ground, get their lives together and it would be perfect for them."

She looked at me and shrugged her shoulders, as if she'd made an embarrassing admission. Then she smiled. "I still have those dreams, right?" she said. "I love the work I'm doing. It kills me to see young people hit rock bottom. They have so much potential."

Her scales, it seemed to me, were in balance.

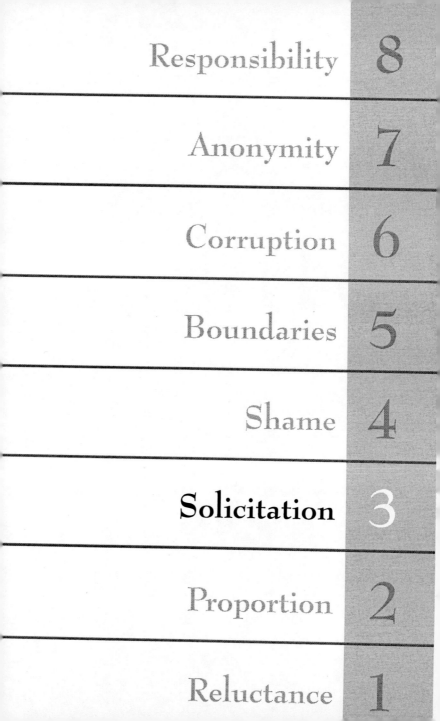

To hand money to the poor after being asked.

P ercy Lane Oliver was a local Red Cross official in London, whose practical solution to an immediate problem resulted in a revolution. Oliver, born in England in 1878, was an assistant librarian and a city employee, but found his calling as a volunteer. During World War I he and his wife helped organize hostels for refugees; after the war he continued his Red Cross work. One evening in 1921 he received an urgent telephone call from a nearby hospital, which needed a blood donor. Oliver rounded up a few colleagues and they went to the hospital together. One of them, a nun, was chosen.

That's how it worked then. Doctors and their patients relied on "donors on the hoof," as walk-in volunteers were called. It was an unreliable system that left a great deal to chance: would a donor with the needed blood type appear at just the right moment?

Inspired by that evening excursion to the hospital, Oliver decided to take the serendipity out of blood donation. He organized a system of volunteers who agreed to register their blood types and be on call for emergencies. It wasn't fancy. The names and numbers were kept on cards; Oliver ran the service out of his parlor. But within five years he had registered 400 people and they responded to more than 700 calls. Eventually, his homemade operation, cobbled together with pragmatism and dedication, developed into England's national blood transfusion service.

I was reminded of Oliver and his unadorned system when my husband received a yellow flyer from the New York Blood Center. "Donate 3 platelet donations between August 28-October 31 and receive a $25 gift card to Applebee's Neighborhood Grill & Bar," it said. The flyer also provided the number to call for an appointment.

There was another telephone number. "Questions, please call Julie Petrosh."

I did call, and found a friendly voice on an answering machine. "If you are eligible for the Border's gift card or the promotional clock, they have not been mailed to donors yet," said Julie Petrosh's recorded message, which then provided a number to make blood appointments as well as her cell phone number. She ended with a cheery, "Thanks and have a great day."

Maimonides places the person who helps *after* being asked on the third level, below the person who simply gives. He was vigilant about protecting the dignity of those in need; they shouldn't have to beg.

His wariness of solicitation has a visceral appeal. Why should we have to be cajoled or nagged? There's a quick answer, the same reason children require nagging and cajoling, even threats and bribes: because we don't always do what we're supposed to do. Rambam praised those who encourage others to give: "He who presses others to give alms and moves them to act thus, his reward is greater than the reward of him who gives alms himself," he wrote. Quoting the Book of Daniel [12:3], he writes: "And they that turn the many to righteousness shall shine as the stars."

Today, however, the solicitation has become not merely a request for help, but a marketing ploy, a sales pitch. It isn't enough to have a worthy cause; you have to offer reciprocity. No tax deduction for giving blood? Have a clock, a meal, a book. It's good for business, good for the blood supply, good for the donor. A charity trifecta.

When Julie Petrosh returned my call, she brushed aside any implicit criticism of those who need extra incentive. "In this day and age people are so busy you have to ask," she said. "The number one reason people give blood is that they get a personal ask. I think people ultimately want to give, whether it's money or blood or time. Their hearts are there but you have to ask." Besides, she pointed out, giving platelets requires a big commitment. While a regular donation takes forty-five minutes start to finish, the platelet gift requires as much as an hour and a half, because the blood is broken into its components, the platelets siphoned off, and the rest given back to the donor.

I felt guilty as I listened to her describe this most direct form of giving, so pure, nothing less than life itself. I did it once and promptly passed out. Low blood pressure. My husband, however, finds giving blood to be a particularly transcendent kind of charity, utterly primal, far more gratifying than writing a check, although he doesn't skimp there. Maybe even a little sexy in its utter intimacy. For a time he gave regularly, but the demands of a new job had kept him away from the blood bank for a while. Hence the flyer, sent to everyone on record who had given blood—or had tried to but been rejected because of a temporary problem like a head cold or a freshly minted tattoo.

The blood bank's promotions hadn't begun as a whim, but in response to another set of rules, the law of supply and demand. Except for the period following September 11, the number of blood donors has been in decline for years. One reason is generational: blood drives had been popularized during the world wars of the twentieth century, and giving blood carried with it overtones of patriotism and good citizenship. That impulse receded in subsequent generations. The AIDS epidemic made people fearful of blood altogether. Then came government rules meant to eliminate the risk that mad cow disease could enter the U.S. blood supply, further shrinking the donor pool.

The promotions are tricky. The blood banks don't want to make them too enticing, encouraging people to falsify their credentials to win the prizes. New York Blood Services limits the amount to $25, just enough to make the donation alluring but not dangerously so. "People are motivated by different reasons," said Petrosh. "Those who donate out of goodness of their heart we thank and those that need a little extra push, we give them that."

Petrosh doesn't mind having to entice people into giving. "The fact that they show up is fantastic," she said. Her job is to make it easy for them to be fantastic. That's why she prefers using chain restaurants for the promotions, places where two people can have lunch for $25. "You can get something for your money," she said.

It isn't necessarily the money, however, that people want, but the feeling that their goodness is being rewarded or appreciated. The New York Blood Center's most successful campaign came in response to a Mother's Day platelet drive; the blood bank sent flowers and chocolates to the mothers of blood donors. Apparently people liked the idea of letting their mothers know they had done a good deed.

Shortly after my conversation with Petrosh, still pondering blood and charity, I remembered a folder on my shelf marked "altruism and vampire bats." I'd been curious to see if the impulse to give had some biological basis, and extended beyond humans. If so, did animals have to be asked? Was solicitation a natural part of the process?

I had been reading studies about vampire bats, whose food source was blood, sipped at night from large animals who had been cut. One of the most frequently mentioned studies came from Gerald Wilkinson, a biology professor at the University of Maryland. He had observed vampire bats in Costa Rica over a period of five years. Wilkinson found that some bats would drink more than they required, and would take the surplus to other bats that had stayed behind—but only when the bats begged for nourishment. That makes evolutionary sense when the bats are related; they are pre-serving their species. But time and again he saw the solicita-tion and donation ritual played out by bats that, although they lived in the same tree hollow or cluster of trees, were not kin. The supplicant bats would lick the lips of the poten-tial donor and the donor would either push them away or sit still and proceed to transfer blood, tongue to mouth.

Wilkinson noticed that the generosity of the unrelated vampire bats seemed to have some strings attached. He found that bats were far more likely to share food with those that had fed them in the past, but not with new bats Wilkinson added to the group he was studying. Females gave; males did not.

Scientists call this kind of behavior "reciprocal altruism," a theory that developed to reconcile generosity displayed by vampire bats and other animals with Darwin's theory of evolution by natural selection. Helping others—especially those who aren't kin—seems at odds with the notion of survival of the fittest. But with animals, as well as humans, giving can have mixed motives. When one chimp offers meat to another who "asks" for it, the gift may be a form of self-protection. When the blood bank offers my husband a $25 "prize" for giving blood, there's an abundance of reciprocal altruism: a new customer for Applebee's, platelets for the blood bank and, for my husband, the satisfaction of giving, and then the pleasure of receiving a reasonably priced meal.

For Maimonides, however, biology wasn't destiny and charitable inclination didn't have to be predetermined. Even if altruism is genetic—and he didn't seem to think that it was—his job was to help improve on the raw material. "Do not imagine that character is determined at birth," he wrote. "We have been given free will. Any person can become as righteous as Moses, or a wicked as Jereboam. We ourselves decide whether to make ourselves learned or ignorant, compassionate or cruel, generous or miserly. No one forces us, no one decides for us, no one drags us along one path or the other; we ourselves, by our own volition, choose our own way." Yet Maimonides was also superstitious, subscribing to the Jewish custom of promising to give charity if God showed mercy. That is not so different from Paolo Alavian's pledge to give his first week's salary to charity upon his first business success.

After fundamentalist Muslims occupied Spain in Rambam's time, Jews were forbidden to practice their religion publicly. Many led a double life, practicing Judaism at home and disguising themselves as Muslims outside, even attending the mosque on holy days. Maimonides' father refused to do this and took his family into exile. They were on the road for years until they settled in Fez, where again Jews were forced to disguise themselves as Muslims. This time Maimonides didn't flee, until a new leader, Abu Yakub Yussaf, began to rule in 1163, and encouraged active persecutions of Jews. Maimonides decided to escape to Palestine with his father, brother, and sisters. After days of traveling by foot, they embarked on a boat for a sea voyage that took about a month. The ship was pummeled by a gut-wrenching storm. Terrified, Maimonides struck a bargain with God; if he survived, he promised to give charity and to order his sons to do the same. They arrived safely. Later, however, Maimonides would learn the futility of the tit-for-tat and the humbling terror of feeling forced to beg. Although he always performed acts of charity whenever his beloved brother, David, embarked on a business trip, the sea eventually swallowed him anyway, on his way to India. Charity didn't forestall tragedy, but suffering left its imprint on Rambam's teachings.

Like every other aspect of giving, then, solicitation isn't simple. It's okay to ask and to offer something in return, but charity can't be a bargaining chip. And while there could be no middleman between Maimonides and his God, in modern philanthropy it helps to have a mediator between those with money and those who need it.

I paid a visit to a master of solicitation, John Rosenwald, the former vice chairman of the securities firm Bear Stearns, who had once been described in *The New York Times* as New York's "poster boy for fund-raising." The article described how he had raised $2.3 billion for huge nonprofit organizations, including the New York University part of the Mount Sinai New York University Medical Center and Health System, the Central Park Conservancy, the Metropolitan Museum of Art, and for his alma maters, Dartmouth and Deerfield Academy. The total would be just under $3 billion when the campaigns he was working on were finished.

After the *Times* piece appeared, Rosenwald was inundated with requests to lecture on philanthropy. He enjoys talking about his salesman's approach to giving and getting. When I called and told him what I was writing about, he invited me to the office he still maintains on Park Avenue.

"I try to shake them up," he said, when I asked him what he tells fundraisers. "To start them thinking along the lines of having to adjust to change. That their world is changing and they don't see it."

He paused and pointed to his computer screen, which he had turned off for our visit. "See that friggin' thing. My life changes every minute. Wall Street! When I turn it back on I find out Bush is in Russia, he says something that got Putin upset, and the market is down 200 points. God forbid. I know about change."

The office, a small space with big views, matched its occupant, a compact man with enormous reserves of energy, self-confidence, and brash charm. At these heights, giving seems theatrical, glamorous, easy.

"I've gotten back so much more than I've given away," he told me. "Not just like when I was chairman of the board of Dartmouth and the Dartmouth singing group in the middle of final exams drove five hours to New York and sang three songs to me."

I sat back in my chair to enjoy the show, occasionally glancing at the various tokens of thanks that decorated his office: the model of the Metropolitan Museum with a big dollar sign out front, the solid gold stethoscope from NYU Medical School, the framed letters of commendation.

Rosenwald saw me looking at his trophies.

"All those things are terrific but on top of that I've been invited on some terrific boards, made wonderful friends whom I wouldn't have met otherwise. I'll be frank to tell you there have been wonderful business benefits. You go on a board and sit down next to the CEO of something or other and the next thing you know, you're doing business together."

Giving has always been good for business; the North American tribal nations called it potlatch when they exchanged gifts to establish diplomatic relations. In the United States, charity and networking were officially linked in 1905, when an attorney named Paul Harris founded the first Rotary Club in Chicago. The idea was to deliberately combine business and pleasure, but when the club made its modest but valuable philanthropic debut—the construction of the city's first public toilet—service was forever added to the mix. Now, Rotary International, located in more than 160 countries, has huge ambitions, including the worldwide vaccination of all children against polio.

Maimonides would have approved, He appreciated the man "who presses others to give alms." But he never specified how hard one should press. Several years ago John Rosenwald and his partner Ace Greenberg began compelling their top brokers to donate a percentage of their earnings to a charity of their choice. But forcing isn't the same thing as asking, and may have the unintended effect of making charity seem like a chore. Rosenwald doesn't see it that way. "Philanthropy is a wonderful habit, but I'm not so sure it's something you're born with," he said. "By forcing people to give a percentage of their income, they see they can give that four percent and still go bowling on Saturday night." He also doesn't mind that the policy turned out to benefit Bear Stearns. "It was better than putting ads in the paper," said Rosenwald. "People talked about us in the most favorable way. 'Those guys may be tough traders, but boy are they charitable, are they philanthropic!'"

Now his full-time business is philanthropy and asking is his art form. Rosenwald is a master of solicitation. For example, he offered the story of the director of a visiting nurse service who came to complain that the organization's board was lethargic, its annual black-tie dinner uninspiring. Rosenwald made this suggestion: "You ever thought of bringing someone whose visiting nurse saved her life? A little old lady who gets up in front of your black-tie dinner?"

His voice got quavery as he put on his old-lady imitation. "I was lying in bed all by myself and my visiting nurse walked in and saved my life."

It was an amusing and effective performance, but the thought nagged at me: Was this the best way to arrange for the care of the elderly and the sick? "You're so good at this," I said truthfully. "But compared with a system where visiting nurses are paid for by the government, and education is paid for by the government, this seems haphazard. You're only going to know about things that are brought to your attention. Isn't there a better way of dealing with the have-nots?"

Rosenwald just shook his head. "I don't know," he said. He's not a philosopher, he's a go-to man. Dwelling on unanswerable questions didn't get him where he is.

"The reality is, I live where I live, I do what I do," he

said. "I come into contact with certain things and go for it." This led to a discussion of how he just went on the board of Teachers College at Columbia University after saying no for five years because Arthur Levine, Teachers College president, asked him. He loved Arthur Levine because Levine told him, "I'm going to throw out all seventeen departments and start all over again."

That was enough for Rosenwald. "He's a brave guy and I want to help him. So I throw myself into that. Now I'm going to get enmeshed in it because I think it's important and because I think he's fabulous and I want to help him. Isn't that what life is about?"

Rosenwald understands that some messages resonate more than others. That there are quality-of-life issues, and then there is life and death.

Two days after September 11 he called Richard Grasso, chairman of the New York Stock Exchange, and asked him to host a breakfast for the Wall Street community working downtown. Rosenwald had been working on a capital campaign to build a new emergency room at NYU Downtown, the old Beekman Hospital. It had been going slowly. The hospital, located on the border of Chinatown and near the Lower East Side, had no special cachet, even though it was also just a few blocks from Wall Street. NYU Downtown didn't cater to high-rent clientele and vice-versa.

Rosenwald's career had been built on his ability to jump

on opportunity. The tragic events that had befallen his city only sharpened those instincts. He understood that on September 11 NYU Downtown became the hospital of choice simply because its emergency room was the closest one to Ground Zero.

He explained his strategy. "So I got the guy who ran the emergency room and said, 'Come to breakfast in your green thing—what do you call it?—scrubs.' We showed slides of an emergency room that normally had thirty-five to forty patients a day that was having nine hundred and with no electricity, no phones. The guy told what it was like, how they did the job. When he finished his little thing with slides I got up and said, 'I know you live in Greenwich but if something like this happens to you at work, this is where you're going to be taken. Will you help us?'"

By the end of breakfast, enough pledges were in to build a new emergency room.

Rosenwald also delights in being the object of a skillful solicitation, appreciating how difficult it can be. Also, he said, how else is he supposed to know what's going on in every corner of the city?

He had bought a table at a charity dinner for Catholic schools because his close friend Tom Murphy, former head of Capital Cities, was being honored. Next thing he knew, he was being invited to breakfast with Cardinal O'Connor, where he met a nun on the Cardinal's staff, who began hounding him to visit one of the scholarship schools.

"Sister Gallagher, with all due respect, I'm up to here in charity," Rosenwald told her. "I love you guys, but I bought the table because of Tom. I'm not committed to this."

She kept calling and calling. Finally he gave in. She picked him up in an ancient Oldsmobile and took him to the worst neighborhood he'd ever seen. Broken glass all over. People sleeping in the streets. Then the front doors opened, children marched out in their little blazers and Rosenthal was hooked. He attended classes all day, learned about how the teachers and principal had managed, in one of the most troubled sections of New York, to achieve an 85 percent graduation rate. Sister Gallagher achieved her purpose: He and his wife "adopted" the school, meaning they agreed to make up its operating deficit.

But, I asked him, was this chance meeting between Sister Gallagher and him, the reliance on her solicitation, the best way to address the imbalance between rich and poor?

"The gap!" he interjected. "The gap is the biggest problem in the world!"

Then he changed the subject, or seemed to, by asking me how I became involved with the Bowery Residents Committee. It was happenstance, I told him: I wanted to become involved in something, a friend told me about the organization, I lived close by.

"Darling girl—can I call you that? You fell into it the

same way," he said triumphantly. "It's one thing to write a check for the 9/11 fund and feel you've done your thing. It's another to engage yourself in addition to writing the check, because the engagement follows a passion."

It occurred to me that passion comes from awareness. Maybe that's the subtext of the third level of giving, the level where one must be asked first. Maimonides was all in favor of solicitation, but he hoped that learning about the person in need would urge the benefactor toward involvement, toward a place where he wouldn't have to be asked.

To hand money to the poor before being asked, but risk making the recipient feel shame.

n 1949, *The New York Times* made a significant change in its annual "Neediest Cases" campaign. For the first time since beginning its Christmas appeal in 1919, the newspaper stopped distinguishing between the "deserving" and the "undeserving" poor.

"What a bleak world it would be if we helped only those who were thoroughly blameless!" wrote an editorialist, explaining the change in policy. "A good many of us make our own bad luck, and we suppose that some of the people represented in the Neediest Cases would not be in trouble now if they had managed their lives differently. It may even be appropriate once in a while, when help is asked, to recall Lord Chesterfield's words: 'Do not refuse your charity even to those who have no merit but their misery.'"

Many conservative thinkers find this benevolent vision symptomatic of everything that's gone wrong with U.S. government policy toward the poor. "The prototypical needy case in the first decades of the appeal was a struggling widow or plucky orphan; today's is more likely to be a single mother of five who finds her welfare check inadequate," wrote Heather MacDonald in *The Burden of Bad Ideas,* a critique of the *Times* and other institutions she regards as liberal.

She continued, "The elite once held the poor to the same standards of behavior that it set for itself: moral character determined the strength of a person's claim for assistance. Those who worked and struggled and yet were overwhelmed by adversity deserved help; the idle and dissolute did not. Over time, though, elite opinion came to see the cause of poverty not in individual character and behavior but in vast, impersonal social and economic forces that supposedly determined individual fate. In response, need became the sole criterion for aid, with moral character all but irrelevant."

Other conservative writers invoke Maimonides in such discussions, focusing on the highest level of the ladder—giving a loan to help people help themselves. They tend to ignore the fourth level, "to hand money to the poor before being asked," which emphasizes the importance of shielding the poor from humiliation. This is a mistake. There's no express elevator to the highest level of giving. To appreciate Rambam's Ladder, you must climb it, rung by rung.

The notion that charity isn't separate from life, but part of it, is echoed in *Forty Hadith of an-Nawawi,* a record of Islamic tradition. "Every person's every joint must perform a charity every day the sun comes up; to act justly between two people is a charity; to help a man with his mount, lifting him onto it or hoisting up his belongings onto it is a charity; a good word is a charity; every step you take in prayers is a charity; and removing a harmful thing from the road is a charity."

Maimonides designed his rules to help people think about giving fairly, not to preempt certain classes of people from receiving help. He didn't even want people to worry about whether they were being taken in by a scam artist. In his treatise "Gifts to the Poor" he stipulates: "If a poor man unknown to anyone comes forth and says, 'I am hungry; give me something to eat,' he should not be examined as to whether he might be an impostor—he should be fed immediately." Significantly, Maimonides specifies that if the amount collected for a poor man exceeds his needs, he gets to keep the surplus.

Perhaps because his family had suffered the humiliation of exile and dispossession, Maimonides was acutely aware of how easy it is to become an outcast. "One must take great care not to shame another in public, whether young or old, either by shameful name-calling or by tale-bearing," he wrote.

There are those, on the other hand, who believe there should be more shame attached to poverty, not less. "Relief, being impersonal and legal, destroys any sense of morality," writes Gertrude Himmelfarb, a conservative scholar. "The donor [the taxpayer] resents his involuntary contribution, and the recipient feels no gratitude for what he gets as a matter of right, which, in any case, he feels to be insufficient."

She invokes the example of the Victorian workhouse in England, whose deterrent effect, she says, stemmed from "the demeaning, degrading fact of being in it." Of course, Himmelfarb demurs, she's not suggesting a revival of workhouses, just their tough-minded philosophy.

Certainly the present welfare system could use reform. Maimonides and his ladder—the whole thing, every step—could provide a useful approach for policy makers. What was he trying to do, after all, but incorporate a system of ethics and morality—of *humanity*—into a system of law?

Rambam's inclination wasn't to blame the poor but to question the way we function as a society. "Do not think you are obliged to repent only for transgressions involving acts, such as stealing, robbing, and sexual immorality," he wrote. "Just as we must repent such acts, so must we examine our evil feelings and repent our anger, our jealousy, our mocking thoughts, our excessive ambition and greed."

Why should poor people in American today feel ashamed about trying to grab at minimal comfort, living in an age of unparalleled excess? "Even the people who are not blessed with big incomes are affected by it," wrote David Brooks, author of *Bobos in Paradise: The New Upper Class and How They Got There.*

"One-sixth of the American population is part of the working poor, earning between $17,000 and $34,000 a year. Many of these people are just scraping by, shopping at Dollar

General, very often without access to banks and health insurance, fearing the next layoff or illness. But still they breathe the air of plenitude. Some get seduced into consumption patterns they cannot afford and fall deeper and deeper into debt. But abundance also means that tomorrow could always be a brighter day."

In Brooks's insouciant reading of contemporary American economics, conceived during a boom time, charity is just another part of the money game, part of the ebb and flow of abundance. "When money comes and goes with such alacrity, it doesn't hurt to give it away," he writes. For the new money classes, it seems, charity is another commodity, something to engage in (or not), but not to be taken too seriously—unless, of course, you happen to be the one who needs it.

My friend Patti Gregory understands this very well. We became friends through our children, who had collided in the park as toddlers, bonded, and then ended up at the same preschool. When I met Patti she had already been in a wheelchair for three years; her son Jack was nine months old when she fell in front of a subway and was left paralyzed.

Patti always arouses much curiosity as she sails around in her wheelchair, a pretty woman wearing an Isaye Miyake dress or something she picked up at a bargain store, stylish either way. Though she is in her early forties, she has the naughty smile of a subversive teenager and, despite her accident, remains slightly reckless, racing against traffic, popping wheelies on curbs. When Patti is around, things happen. She approaches life as an experiment, constantly testing new hair colors and new theories. I'd come to learn that she dispenses wisdom in most unusual ways. So when she told me to meet her at Bruno's Bakery for coffee because she had something to say about charity (she knew I was writing a book on the subject), I left home immediately.

On my way to Bruno's I saw "my" homeless man standing at the corner of a busy intersection. I began to veer in another direction, hoping he wouldn't see me, in part because I was eager to see Patti but also to avoid the guilty feelings he stirred up in me. My attempt at circumvention was hopeless and ridiculous. There was too much traffic to get very far.

"Hey there," he called out. "You don't have to walk away if you don't want to give me money."

Caught! Sheepishly I walked over and retrieved a small shred of dignity by not protesting.

"Look at this," he said with a smile, showing no sign of insult. He pulled a coin out of his pocket, and made it disappear out of one hand only to reappear in the other. He pulled a quarter from behind my ear and grinned.

"You know my name," he said, as if he was taunting me with the ladder of charity itself, which gave high ranking to anonymity between giver and receiver.

"David," I said. By then we had introduced ourselves.

He nodded. "That's right." And then he told me his entire name—first, middle, last.

So much for anonymity, though my cheeks were indeed burning with shame.

"My name is Julie," I said, thinking he had forgotten.

"I know," he replied, and then wished me a Happy Day, Darling, and waved good-bye. No money changed hands.

Patti was waiting for me at Bruno's. Her hair was an exuberant red that day. When I told her about my encounter with David she generously offered a parallel story. She told me about a man named Matthew who hangs out in her neighborhood in a wheelchair, selling batteries and audiotapes. He is a street person; she is married to an advertising executive and had a career in the fashion business. But because they are both disabled, Matthew has felt comfortable talking to her about their common experience, and she feels obligated to him for similar reasons. Now, even if she's in a rush or not in the mood, she finds it difficult to avoid him.

For Patti, giving (and taking) has become not so much a matter of choice or ethics but of necessity. There are too many sidewalks without graduated curbs at street crossings; unwieldy door entrances to negotiate; items placed beyond her reach in stores. Sometimes, because she is self-reliant and refuses to acknowledge these obstacles, she tries to manage by herself, falls out of her wheelchair, and then needs help getting back in. She doesn't have the freedom to choose anonymity; she has become a public person, an object of curiosity, concern, and fear: How did someone who looks so insouciant, so *normal,* end up in a wheelchair? She knows she has no reason to feel ashamed, but it's almost an inevitable reaction in a culture that places a premium on independence and fortitude.

"When I'm out on the street, I represent this thing that has been damaged, this life that has been damaged. For a while I was angry that I needed help and didn't want to rely on other people or to be their good deed for the day," said Patti. "I worried that maybe they'd done mean stuff to people or evil things at their job and then helping this woman in a wheelchair would bring them good karma. People actually say to me, 'That'll be my good deed for the day.' That made me feel like they were using me in some way."

For Patti, the corruption of charity, and the shame in it, isn't monetary but personal, most dangerous to the recipient when a gift is used as leverage. "If someone gives you help financially or physically, the next step can be that maybe you owe them something. You have to be very careful of that and don't want to put yourself into that position even if you are able to accept the fact that you need help," she told me.

If Maimonides was bent on reconciling faith and reason in his quest for righteousness, Patti has been determined to find symbiosis between the giving and the taking. This seemed to me the most viable interpretation of the fourth level, where the poor person doesn't have to ask for help. Putting a shield of anonymity between giver and recipient is one way of warding off shame. But showing respect is another. "You have to take those moments when you can make someone's day or life or situation a little better without having an ulterior motive," she said. "The more our collective consciousness sees things that way the better we will get at doing random acts of kindness."

We stopped talking long enough to admire the rows of pastry behind glass, hungry window-shoppers, and decided to split a little lemon tart. That's another thing I love about Patti. She doesn't even try to resist temptation. Fortified, Patti told me the story she wanted me to hear.

Six months after her accident, she had decided to become a volunteer at "God's Love We Deliver," an organization whose volunteers take food to people so sick with AIDS they can't leave their homes.

For Patti, who had been a fashion stylist, accustomed to jetting off to Japan to scope out new trends, volunteering was her way back into the world. She was sick of pep talks from her friends and family, trying to convince her that her life could be exactly as it had been. But she didn't feel capable of going back to work, as many had encouraged her to do, or competing in the disabled Olympics, which she felt many wanted her to do—as if everyday life wasn't putting enough hurdles in her path.

Although the spinal cord damage had physically discon-
nected only her lower half, her sense of dislocation went
much further. Patti is a free spirit; that's what brought her to
New York from Ohio in the first place. Now, trapped by her
own body, but unwilling to succumb to despair, she had to
regroup. She had undergone months of physical therapy
aimed at giving her as much independence as possible, but
she realized that there would always be times when she
would have to ask for help. This disturbed her—that old saying, "I'm not a charity case," had taken on a whole new
meaning for her. So rather than consider herself a charity
case, she decided to volunteer, something she'd been meaning to do but had never had the time for.

She worked as a receptionist at God's Love. Then someone asked her if she would mind conducting interviews for a
video the agency was making to attract volunteers, a kind of
infomercial. This appealed to Patti, a natural talker and an
even better listener. One of her interview subjects was Ganga
Stone, the agency's founder.

Patti was already familiar with the well-publicized story
of how Stone began God's Love We Deliver, which had
become a fashionable charity in New York during the AIDS
crisis of the late twentieth century. In fact, the founder's story
was one of the things—apart from convenient location and
hours—that drew Patti to God's Love We Deliver. Stone was

a compulsive searcher, moving from radical feminist politics to the Buddhism of an ashram in India, eventually ending up as a hospice volunteer in New York. Her revelation came the day a young man dying of AIDS threw the groceries she'd brought him on the floor. He was too weak to cook. Stone went through his address book and organized a schedule with his friends, so that every meal would be taken care of. From this she developed God's Love We Deliver, whose volunteers prepared meals and took them where they were needed. There was a practicality and directness in Stone's approach that was very appealing to wary New Yorkers. Stone's revelation had become legendary in certain circles of New York, attracted by her Buddhist-Jewish-Christian-Hindu philosophy, her cause, and her ability to inspire wealthy donors—and not so wealthy ones as well.

Patti already felt a connection when she called Stone to ask her the prepared questions for the video. When Stone had finished answering the questions, Patti didn't want to get off the phone. She wanted the bond to be reciprocal, for Stone to appreciate that Patti was helping other people despite her own trauma, which was still fresh. She wanted Stone to be impressed that it wasn't just anyone interviewing her about her experiences but someone who had also suffered. So when Stone seemed to be finished talking, Patti blurted out that she had had an accident six months earlier, that she was paralyzed, that she had to use a wheelchair.

Stone's response shocked her. Instead of partaking in a mutual admiration society (Patti's secret hope) and telling Patti how extraordinary and brave she was for helping others despite her own hardship, Stone said, "That's such a gift that you've gotten."

Patti wondered if she'd misheard. A gift? It seemed like such a strange thing to say, almost insulting if not sadistic. Yet there came a time when Patti realized that there was truth, at least some truth, in Stone's words. She eventually believed that if someone like that—someone whom she admired—believed something could be gained from this terrible new state of being, perhaps a new way of looking at the world, then maybe it was possible. But she also believed that if almost anyone else had said the same thing about her disability she would have thought that person was monumentally insensitive or really stupid.

"It was such an unusual response," Patti said, "the first time someone had seen the tragedy of my situation as something that could enrich my life. It took a while but it gave me strength to think that I might gain from this experience—and I have as I've matured in this condition of being disabled in the world. I see things I wouldn't have seen before."

Patti's words were on my mind the next time I saw David, back in front of the grocery store. This time I crossed the street to approach him. I had five dollars in my pocket and just handed it to him. He thanked me.

I had been thinking obsessively about Maimonides' admonition against shaming the recipient of charity. Hesitating a minute—had David now become a research project?—I asked him how he felt about taking the money from me.

He didn't hesitate a bit.

"I feel lucky," he said.

I laughed, relieved to hear this honest answer to my earnest question. Still, I pressed on. "Do you feel ashamed at all?"

"Not really," he said. "This is what I do."

That stopped me for a minute. Did he mean begging was his occupation; my gift actually wages?

"You mean, like your job?" I asked.

He looked a little impatient. "No, it's not my job," he said. "I have a business."

I was wishing I hadn't started this conversation. Did I think my handout entitled me to this kind of probing with someone who might be mentally unbalanced?

David continued. "I do feel bad having to ask for money but when my leg is better I'm going to work. This life isn't for me."

I must have looked worried because he said, "I don't mean I'm going to kill myself or anything like that. I mean I'm going to go into business."

"What kind of work?" I asked him, not seriously. I felt he

must be delusional.

"Tube socks," he said.

"Tube socks?" I repeated.

And then he told me how he could buy socks wholesale on Orchard Street and take them around in a cart and sell them. Tube socks! I'd seen plenty of men selling them on the street and his description of how the business worked seemed knowledgeable.

Suddenly my handout felt like seed money, a small business loan. Had it become more virtuous?

David vanished for a couple of months. I thought of him from time to time, fantasizing that he'd set up shop in midtown, where pedestrian traffic was steady and tube sock need was great. Then he reappeared near my house empty-handed—no cart, no tube socks. When I saw him back on the corner, unencumbered, I felt disappointed, even though I understood that small businesses tend to fail, and his was most tenuous.

Of course, I'd suspected all along there was another explanation apart from the press of business for his absence. It had been a sweltering summer and he might have been holed up somewhere with air-conditioning. I knew the drop-in center at the Bowery Residents' Committee filled up on hot days.

He was limping a little, wearing a light blue T-shirt and a blue scarf around his head. He seemed even thinner than usual.

"I'm glad to see you," I said and meant it. I confess I have a superstitious streak and felt his reappearance was a good sign, but I was also simply relieved to see him.

"Good to see you, darling," he said, and then told me he'd been sick, some kind of stomach infection.

"I'm ashamed to say it," he said, "but sometimes when I don't get money I do dig around in garbage cans and I must have eaten something that made me sick."

This sounded like a confession. He looked terrible, wasted.

"I was throwing up and couldn't stop," he said. "I ended up in the hospital."

Without him asking, I pulled out my wallet and gave him a five-dollar bill, which had been tucked between some ones and a few twenties. Why didn't I give him a twenty?

He took the money matter-of-factly and said thank you, and then put out his hand, which I shook. His grip was firm—a lot firmer than mine.

To give to someone you don't know, but allow your name to be known.

O ne day following a board meeting of the Bowery Residents Committee, I received a disturbing telephone call from one of the more generous board members.

"Do you know how many of our clients are illegals?" he asked sharply.

It took me a couple of seconds to comprehend his meaning. He was asking about undocumented noncitizens, illegal aliens. "No, I don't," I replied slowly, so I could figure out where the conversation had come from and where it might be going. I replayed the board meeting, which had been at BRC's Senior Center, where meals and various recreational and social services programs are offered to elderly homeless people.

I have a soft spot for the Senior Center; I began working in the soup kitchen there in the late 1980s as a volunteer. After lunch I'd hang around with the old men—most of them were men—and listen to their hard luck stories, finding echoes of John Steinbeck and Woody Guthrie, maybe because I wanted to. I also helped deliver meals to the nearby flophouses, terrible dark holes where men lived in cages, four walls with a chicken-wire ceiling to let in air. In row after row, the windowless construction maximized the number of cubicles that could be fitted in, and that maximized the profit: Landlords received $10 a night for each one. The men stayed in the flops because they were too sick or shook up to leave. Many of them were Chinese who had never learned English; they spent most of their lives on the Bowery, back when it wasn't fit to be anything other than a last stop. It had never occurred to me to ask them for their papers.

At the board meeting, the question had come up: Did the BRC extend help to undocumented people? The director, an immigrant from Vietnam, looked surprised, then politely said yes, though she didn't know how many people fell into that category. A tiny percentage, at any rate.

That seemed to be that. But it wasn't. Apparently the board member who had called me had been stewing about it all night.

"How can I give my money to people who aren't even citizens when we have plenty of real Americans who need help?" he said.

I tried to disarm him with a story about my Uncle Louis, oldest of seven children in a Hungarian-Jewish farm family, who came to this country illegally as a young man and never got around to getting his papers. His children—

and grandchildren—all became good, tax-paying citizens. When my story was met with silence, I turned businesslike and assured him I'd find out how many people were affected and where the policy had come from.

Easy enough: The New York City Human Rights Law, one of the most comprehensive civil rights laws in the country, includes noncitizens as a protected class of people. In other words, social service agencies which, like the BRC, receive city funding can't discriminate for a variety of reasons, including race, age, gender, and citizenship status. I reported back to the board member, who told me he'd have to decide what he was going to do about it.

Because I didn't want to antagonize him, I refrained from asking the question I wanted answered: Why did it matter so much to him? And why, Uncle Louis aside, who never took government or charity money as far as I know, didn't it matter to me? What are the boundaries? Who is a stranger?

Maimonides placed the person who gives without knowing who is receiving the money above the person who has to be solicited. In addition, he explicitly specified that strangers should not be excluded from gifts set aside for the poor. After all, he knew what it was to be a stranger, since he was an outsider in every country in which he lived, including Palestine, which was then under Christian rule.

This doesn't mean that Rambam didn't discriminate: "A poor man who is one's relative has priority over all others," he wrote. "The poor of one's own household have priority over the other poor of his city, and the poor of his city have priority over the poor of another city." Even so, his commentary admirably presses for fairness, albeit fairness administered with a pragmatic touch. Discussing why it is important to help poor people from outside your community, even potential enemies, he observes that such righteous behavior is necessary "for the sake of the ways of peace." Philanthropy as diplomacy.

Philosopher Peter Singer, writing almost a millennium later, dealt directly with the issue of boundaries in his provocative book *Practical Ethics.* Many people loathe Singer for his utilitarian views on euthanasia and for his unwillingness to differentiate human beings from other animals. But I admire his insistence on carrying a moral debate to its uncomfortable extremes, his refusal to accept complacency, his Rambamlike moral obsessiveness.

In a chapter called "Rich and Poor," Singer begins with the question of boundaries. Quoting Robert McNamara, former president of the World Bank, Singer invokes the term "absolute poverty" to distinguish the dire conditions in countries like Ethiopia from the comparatively comfortable situation of people living below the poverty line in Britain or the United States. In McNamara's words, absolute poverty is "a condition of life so characterized by malnutrition, illiteracy, disease, squalid surroundings, high infant mortality and

low life expectancy as to be beneath any reasonable definition of human decency."

Singer then creates a contrapuntal category of "absolute
affluence," which he defines as those who are able to buy
basic necessities of life and still have money left over for lux-
uries. He points out the tiny percentage of gross national
product that the richest countries give to the poorest. "If
these are the facts, we cannot avoid concluding that by not
giving more than we do, people in rich countries are allowing those in poor countries to suffer from absolute poverty,
with consequent malnutrition, ill health, and death," he
writes. "This is not a conclusion that applies only to governments. It applies to each absolutely affluent individual, for
each of us has the opportunity to do something about the
situation; for instance, to give our time or money to voluntary organizations like Oxfam, Care War on Want, Freedom
from Hunger, Community Aid Abroad, and so on."

He engages in a series of ethical tests. He asks, for example, if by failing to help the absolutely poor the absolutely
affluent are engaging in a kind of genocide. He asks whether
there is a moral distinction between omission and commis-
sion, and how far the obligation to assist must be extended.
Yet after performing a philosophical high wire act, his actual
advice on how much to give (if not precisely to whom) falls
back on the Biblical standby, the tithe, as a minimum.

Singer's global view of responsibility is more Anglo than

American (he is an Australian). Reading *Practical Ethics* reminded me of how many times during my interviews, especially with foundation people, I was told that Americans are far more generous than any other nationality. Hosts of reasons were offered: the Protestant ethic, Jewish teachings, the Catholic influence, capitalism and its emphasis on individual achievement, even something inherent in democracy itself. None of this is quantifiable, but indicates that the American desire to think of ourselves as essentially benevolent is widespread.

Karen Wright, a researcher at the London School of Economics, argued in a compelling paper, "Generosity versus Altruism," that Americans may be more generous but are not necessarily more altruistic. They give more money, but they also have more to give. Americans also take a bottom-line approach, wanting to know results, effect, and, often, how giving to others will make our lives better. "Americans believe in giving to needs that they can directly see, feel, and understand," Wright contends in her comparison of philanthropy and charity in the United States and the United Kingdom. The bulk of charitable contributions in the U.S. goes to religion and higher education: 38 percent and 15 percent, respectively, of total gifts in 2001. In the U.K, international aid received the largest chunk of charity, about 25 percent.

Wright distinguishes between the "generosity" of Americans and the "altruism" of the British. "U.S. giving is heavily interlaced with self-interest, either directly through tax benefits, benefits from the supported charity, or social status; or indirectly through the achievement of social goals which one might desire, such as better child care, civil rights, better parks, etc. Moreover these self-interested motivations are not only acceptable, but are socially approved," she writes. "Giving is seen as an expression of personal and social identity and goals."

By contrast, she says, "The British expect that giving should be altruistic, even self-sacrificing." Unlike Americans, who prefer organized philanthropy, the British prefer the spare-change method, according to Wright. When they donate through organizations, they tend to choose universal causes such as Oxfam or Save the Children, which benefit them neither directly nor indirectly. "For the British, moral motivation is deeply rooted in collective duty, a concept that would be quite foreign to Americans," concludes Wright.

What is the bottom line in this comparison? People in the United States give at a rate more than twice that of Great Britishers. Yet about the same percentage of people, somewhere between two thirds and three quarters, give something in both countries. Wright also points out that the religious and educational institutions that dominate American giving—institutions that benefit themselves-are not deemed charitable in the U.K.

Thomas Murphy, retired chairman of Capital

Cities/ABC (now a Disney subsidiary), used to believe that charity begins and ends at home, or at least in the neighborhood. He learned about helping people from his father, a New York State judge in Brooklyn, who specialized in brokering favors. When Murphy began running a little UHF television station in Albany New York, someone told him he needed to get involved in the community. Good for business. So he went on the board of the local Boys Club.

When he returned to New York as the head of a major media company, that belief in community involvement still held; he was just operating in a much bigger community. He joined the board of the New York University Medical Center, where he would remain for thirty-five years, and became involved in the Madison Girls and Boys Club. He also sent money to Harvard Business School, not because he thought the place needed the money but because he felt loyalty to the institution that he believed was instrumental in his career trajectory. And he gave to the Catholic Church, specifically directing a large portion of his giving to the inner city scholarship fund sponsored by the archdiocese.

Upon retiring from his corporate job, Murphy unexpectedly turned his attention abroad, to places he had never really thought about before. He became chairman of Save the Children, the foundation that invites donors to "sponsor" a child in a poor country, often in the absolute poverty zone—the war, famine, and flood zone. "When I retired I thought I'd do some traveling, but I thought it would be to places like London and Paris," he told me when I visited him in his elegant chairman-emeritus office at ABC. "Now it's been Mozambique and Mali and Vietnam and Pakistan. It's a very sobering experience and I really admire the not-for-profit people who work for Save the Children. They're dedicated, intelligent, hardworking and do a lot of things I could never possibly do because I'm so spoiled."

What made him change so abruptly from local to distant charity?

"I got talked into it by Bill Haber," he said, referring to the man who once ran Creative Artists Agency, the big Hollywood talent firm, with Michael Ovitz. When the high-flying agency got its comeuppance in the business, Haber quit and then went off to do good deeds back East. He volunteered the way dealmakers do; he said he'd bring the organization a chairman who could raise money. Murphy, an old friend, had proved that he could do that.

"He took me around," said Murphy, when I asked him what clinched it for him. "First to the Middle East for a week, to Jordan, to Lebanon—there are a lot of Palestinian refugee children there—and to Gaza and the West Bank," he said. "We went to the Mississippi Delta to see poor people here in the United Sates, and to the Navaho Nation in Arizona. He talked me into thinking I could be of help."

Asked why he gives, Murphy answered immediately that

it came from his parents, their example, and from his Catholic upbringing. Whatever the reason, he had the contacts and wherewithal and emotional flexibility to extend his notion of community. Yet there are all kinds of definitions for "community" and "stranger," and a variety of ways to map meaningful charitable boundaries.

That became apparent to me during a conversation with Marnie Pillsbury. I'd initially arranged a meeting with her because she'd been managing David Rockefeller's personal giving for the last twelve years. It is a job to which she is well suited as the granddaughter of a Presbyterian minister, and the daughter and wife of wealthy men whose money came from corporations that produced comfort foods (Quaker Oats and Pillsbury products). She'd spent most of her life trying to prove to herself that she wasn't, as she put it, simply a rich blonde super-WASP content to luxuriate in the privilege to which she'd been born.

Pillsbury is a small woman with a friendly smile who walked fast as she guided me to a small conference room on the fifty-sixth floor of Rockefeller Center one sunny afternoon. We zoomed past an exquisite collection of art, and settled in to talk in front of a window with a magnificent view of the city that has been critically shaped by Rockefeller money and influence.

These days, Bill Gates's fortune and philanthropy have eclipsed the Rockefellers' in dollar amount, but the family's legacy is a crucial part of America's philanthropic history. The fortune they earned in the nineteenth century by exploiting workers and engaging in cutthroat business practices was put through the purifying process of philanthropy in the twentieth. The Rockefellers think long and hard about their giving and do it very differently from one another. Even now, Pillsbury explained, David links his philanthropy to deductible income, while his brother Lawrence is more intuitive and emotional.

But it turned out to be Pillsbury's own experience, which she discussed incidentally, that was most instructive that day. "I used to think I knew the good guys and the bad guys," she told me wistfully. It was a beautiful spring morning; the news out of the Middle East, as usual, had been bad. "Now I don't know anymore. I worry deeply that we Americans don't understand the rest of the world, so I'm on the board of an organization called World Learning that's spending a great deal of time on that."

She nodded toward the skyline outside. We were facing south. "They're not there anymore," she said. We sat in silence and then she assured me she hadn't forgotten what we had been talking about: how people decide to give and to whom. She said the terrorist attacks on the World Trade Center had changed her boundaries, as well as her urge to see past them. "What motivates me are transformations, little ones and big ones, anything I do that can make something a little different, a little better. My need to feel connections is very strong. Even if I'm on a bus and I have some interaction with someone, for me it's a little transformation, it's a little change."

For most of us, this desire for connection is a crucial component of our giving. We may like the idea of saving the world but find it more practical, and emotionally rewarding, to pursue the little transformations: to volunteer at the local hospital, to drop by and say hello to an elderly neighbor.

Maimonides didn't directly discuss the question of boundaries, whether to give globally or locally. It isn't likely that the idea would have occurred to many people of his time. But even his more convoluted rules contain suggestions for thinking about giving today. In his discussion of the fifth level of giving, for example, Rambam invokes the example of the wise men who would put money in a folded sheet, then throw it over their shoulders so poor people could pluck out coins as the wise men strolled down the street. The idea, again, was to protect the poor from humiliation, the assumption being that the wise men wouldn't peek over their shoulders. It's hard to imagine how the image conjured by this scenario forestalls shame, Maimonides makes his point, though. It is necessary to go to great lengths—even preposterous ones—to protect the giving exchange.

New York is a relatively compact city, vertical instead of horizontal. Geographic distances are small; social gaps enormous. It's an easy subway ride from the indisputable, absolute affluence of the Rockefeller offices to the relative poverty that still exists on the Lower East Side. That's where I met Misha Avramoff, director of Project Ezra, an organization that helps elderly Jews who didn't take part in the exodus uptown or to the suburbs, and have missed out on the area's gentrification.

These elderly poor represent a different kind of stranger. They are not "us," but rather who we might become, or who we might have been. That's another lesson to be learned from Rambam's careful protection of the needy: It is essential that we acknowledge the stranger within ourselves.

Avramoff's tiny office, located at the end of a cinder block hallway, is dedicated to the notion of never forgetting. It is crowded with pictures of middle-European Jews from the past and stacks of coffee cans, waiting to be distributed to his clients. There is no shutting out the din of the old people having lunch and the volunteers gossiping noisily in the halls, nor, I sensed, would Avramoff want to feel apart from it.

A small man in his early sixties, with gray hair and mischievous eyes, he seemed satisfied with the path he'd chosen. He was born in Bulgaria in 1939 and, having managed to avoid the Nazi death camps, immigrated to Israel with his family in 1949. Avramoff then came to the United States, where he studied philosophy at Columbia University in the rare moments he wasn't outside the university walls protesting for civil rights, and against the military-industrial establishment.

"I needed to be needed. I get too angry," he said calmly. "I am exceedingly angry at certain injustices. In the 1960s it was much easier because you were there with 100,000 others and yelled and screamed and occasionally we middle-class people, we got arrested—only to be released again. I slowly came to the conclusion that life is comprised of small victories. So I still dream of revolutions but I no longer partake in anything like that. Day by day now, I visit an elderly person. I get some money so I can get food for those that need to stretch the Social Security checks. These are the small victories."

Having given up on repairing the entire universe, he decided to see if he could help brighten the last months or years of the indigent old people on the Lower East Side. He began Project Ezra with some friends, and decided at the outset that they would remain independent of the government and large charity machines like the Federation of Jewish Philanthropies. They refused to buy lists or participate in any modern fundraising techniques, except to issue a report twice a year to Project Ezra supporters, many of whom send in $5 a year. Instead, Avramoff spoke about his constituency at any synagogue or club that would have him. When the Internet developed, Project Ezra was posted on the Web.

This word-of-mouth grassroots operation raises $550,000 a year, which is spent on food and various programs, like one that brings medical students to Project Ezra to find out what it's like to be old. The agency has a van with a hydraulic lift for wheelchairs, to bring people in for various activities. Sometimes, to help his clients break their isolation, Avramoff takes them on field trips, often to suburban synagogues. "It's nice to see a very successful lawyer who probably makes in a year what they made in a lifetime behind a sewing machine sitting together," said Avramhoff. "That's a community. For our people it alleviates the loneliness. For the people who volunteer to host us they're doing something beyond sending a check."

For him, the boundaries of giving are narrow, and charity occurs one-to-one, though he doesn't like the word charity, preferring *tzedakah,* and its root, *tzedek,* justice. "Justice to me is give if you can, take if you need—not only money, but whatever it is you have something of," he said. "The Jewish community has adopted the American creed, replacing the individual in *tzedakah* with big organizations acting on behalf of individuals."

Sometimes, he said, you have to look in the face of a stranger to find your own soul—and if that breaks the rule about not knowing to whom you are giving, so be it. His fervor and idealism, though tempered these days, resonated with quiet power. "In our quest to build the powerful institutions we have gotten away from the notion of I and thou, me and God, of Martin Buber," he said, referring to yet another great philosopher and theologian. "We've moved to the corporate kind of charity giving, which is fine, but it should never replace the individual notion of feeling a responsibility to participate." Things were becoming clearer. On Rambam's Ladder I was finding the panoramic view, a place to take in the vast and varied boundaries of the human heart.

To give to someone you know, but who doesn't know from whom he is receiving help.

All the ingredients for a morality tale about charity gone astray were contained in the story of Clara Hale, who founded Hale House, a children's shelter in New York City's Harlem, and her daughter Lorraine, who looted it.

According to Hale House legend, as constructed by the Hales themselves, the charity officially began in 1969, when Lorraine Hale—then a first-grade teacher—stopped at a red light at the corner of Amsterdam Avenue and 146th Street. She noticed a homeless woman, apparently high on drugs, sitting on a crate holding a bundle of rags.

As Hale would recall in a history she cowrote to celebrate Hale House's thirtieth anniversary: "In that instant, I saw something—a tiny hand—reaching out from that bundle." She began to drive away, but then returned to the woman. "Do you know my mother? Mrs. Hale?" she asked the woman. "She lives over there," and she gave her mother's address to the woman. Within weeks, twenty-two babies made their way to Clara Hale's apartment. Soon she would become known as "Mother Hale," provider of last resort for babies whose mothers were addicts or imprisoned.

Clara Hale had always taken in foster children; Lorraine grew up in an apartment crowded with cradles and was expected to help with her mother's charges from an early age. But Hale House became a government-approved charity, and would develop into a multimillion dollar enterprise, lauded for its self-help ethos, and possibly for its punitive attitude toward the children's mothers. Hale House was embraced by celebrities and politicians as well as by people who sent checks for $5. In 1985, President Ronald Reagan invited Mother Hale to be his guest at the State of the Union address, called her an "American heroine," and awarded her the Presidential Medal of Freedom. When she died in 1992, her daughter Lorraine took over.

Two years later, the *New York Daily News* conducted an investigation of Hale House and found a tabloid-worthy story. The reporters, Heidi Evans and Dave Saltonstall, described a horrific picture of roach infestation and under-staffing, haphazardly arranged adoptions, and medical care provided by an unlicensed doctor.

The juiciest morsel in the stew, however, was Lorraine Hale, wayward heir to her mother's legacy. She had turned out to be an even more effective fundraiser than her mother, partly through necessity. In 1990, even before Clara Hale died, the administration of Mayor David Dinkins had stopped contracting with Hale House and similar group shelters, believing that kind of care was not in the best interest of young children. Subsequently Hale House was no longer subjected to the audits that accompany government funding.

Lorraine Hale became something of an icon herself. As a spokeswoman for a philosophy of "tough love," she gained national prominence with an appearance on ABC's *Nightline*. In the nine years following her mother's death, she pulled in $43 million for the children of Hale House, or so she said.

From the funds she raised to help children, she bought a top of the line Jacuzzi, renovated her home in suburban Scarsdale, and invested $500,000 in *Faith Journey*, an off-Broadway musical meant to celebrate Martin Luther King Jr., produced by her husband, Jesse DeVore. (Perhaps even more disgraceful than the Hale House scandal in status-conscious New York, the play was a flop, described by Ben Brantley in *The New York Times* as "dispiritingly listless and confused.") Instead of using two apartment buildings she was given to house troubled mothers, she rented them to middle-class people and kept the profits. The person who was listed as Hale House treasurer, who should have been in charge of oversight, had died five years before Lorraine Hale's unseemly expenditures were uncovered. It appeared that another financial person, whose name appeared as cosigner on checks with Hale, was entirely fictitious.

The scandal provoked editorial harrumphing as well as a

touch of gleefulness at yet another revelation of human falli-
bility lurking beneath a public display of piety. "Lorraine
Hale allegedly used nearly $1.3 million in Hale House dona-
tions as her personal piggy bank," chortled the *News*. Hale
and her husband eventually pleaded guilty in exchange for
five years probation rather than prison. (The prosecutor cited
their ages—she was seventy-six, he seventy—as the reason
for the leniency.) Hale House continues to exist; its new
executive director claims the scandal hasn't tarnished the
memory of Clara Hale.

Anonymity is not, as commonly believed, the highest
form of giving. Maimonides reserved highest praise for the
person who hands someone a gift or loan, or enters into a
partnership, or otherwise helps out in a way designed to offer
the recipient financial independence. Still, he was punctilious
about anonymity; three of the eight levels elaborate on the
importance of shielding recipient from giver or vice versa.
While Rambam's Ladder doesn't deal directly with fraud or
theft, Maimonides used anonymity as the metaphoric dam,
protecting not so much the recipient or the benefactor, but
the process itself from being overwhelmed by a flood of
human frailty. After all, the stream of righteousness, being
especially pure, is especially vulnerable to contamination.

Rambam suggested the institution of a "Chamber of
Secrets" in the temple—the equivalent of a mutual fund for
charity—where people could leave anonymous gifts. By

encouraging the use of a middleman acting as a buffer, he anticipated the temptation that would ruin Lorraine Hale. Yet he warned that people should contribute to this fund only if the people in charge of it were trustworthy. If they were not, he urged people to deposit sums of money directly at the doorsteps of the poor. That's the sixth level, where the donor knows who is receiving the gift, but the poor person doesn't know who is giving it.

The Hale House saga falls in the sixth level, where compromises are made. The wealthy man is forced to know to whom he is giving because the people tending the alms have been misbehaving. Complete anonymity is sacrificed to make sure the job gets done.

It has become easier to make sure that middlemen are doing their jobs properly, and that contributions end up at the proper doorstep. In 1999, a nonprofit organization called Philanthropic Research began posting charities' annual tax returns on the Internet. Anyone can check to see how much a charity spends on fund-raising or administration, and how much goes to the cause it supports; how much goes to services and how much to salaries.

Now, though, there are also more subtle kinds of corruption to consider. The cult of personality—the antithesis of selfless anonymity—has become a significant aspect of charity. Rock stars routinely gather to raise millions for various causes; professional fund-raisers promise potential donors

their spot of immortality—a building, a chair, a hall, a tree—
if they'll just give money. The secular deification of Clara
Hale didn't necessarily lead her daughter to commit fraud,
but did it help encourage her? Is a gift less worthy because
the donor wants a public show of appreciation? Does it matter if it takes a celebrity endorsement to encourage some
people to give?

Are acts of charity diminished by inappropriate behavior
that's entirely separate from the generous behavior? After A.
Alfred Taubman, the Detroit real estate developer and former
chairman of Sotheby's, was convicted for price-fixing, his
hometown newspaper, the *Detroit News,* ran a poll on its Web
site asking readers how they thought Taubman would be
remembered: for his conviction for price-fixing, or for his
mall development and philanthropy?

No contest. Fifty-nine percent of the respondents said
price-fixing; 40 percent said philanthropy.

Six weeks after the World Trade Center attack, the president of the American Red Cross, Dr. Bernadine Healy, was
forced out of her job. She had been criticized for collecting
too much blood, more than was needed at the time. People
were also upset that the $500 million collected by The Liberty
Fund, the Red Cross's 9/11 collection, wasn't distributed
only to victims but to a variety of Red Cross services.

Yet personal unpopularity seemed to have as much to do
with Dr. Healy's departure as politics. In subsequent reports,

it appeared that Dr. Healy's blunt style and impolitic determination to shake up the Red Cross didn't sit well with colleagues. She insisted that her resignation was provoked by her support for including Israel in the International Red Cross.

As I read about the nasty politicking at the Red Cross I recalled part of a conversation with Tracey Capers, a consultant to nonprofit organizations, who had begun her career working in them: "People working in charitable organizations or government can be some of the most ruthless, arrogant, obnoxious people. The charitable environment is not always charitable," she said. "When I first started working in the not-for-profit world I thought these were going to be utopian Sally Sunshines, but they'll just tear your eyes out to get to the top."

When I asked her whether this behavior diminished the process, Capers shrugged. "They're still doing good work."

Take this inquiry a step further: After the September 11 attack on the United States, governments all over the world began cracking down on Islamic charities accused of being linked to various terrorist organizations. The most notorious case in the U.S. involved the Holy Land Foundation for Relief and Development, incorporated in Texas. The foundation's charter says it is dedicated to "charitable relief for refugees and the indigent needy" Palestinians living in the West Bank and Gaza. In December 2001, the U.S. government froze the foundation's assets, saying that it was a front for Hamas, the Islamic Resistance Movement, begun in 1988. The founding covenant of Hamas specifically states as a central goal the destruction of the state of Israel.

Did the Holy Land Foundation give money to schools and widows and orphans?

Yes.

But the Holy Land Foundation also apparently supported the military and political goals of Hamas, whose covenant approvingly quotes The Prophet: "The Day of Judgement will not come about until Moslems fight the Jews (killing the Jews), when the Jew will hide behind stones and trees. The stones and trees will say O Moslems, O Abdulla, there is a Jew behind me, come and kill him."

Making contributions to such ends can't be righteous giving.

What about when the link between charity and war is made in the name of self- defense? The United Jewish Appeal (UJA) was begun in 1935 to give aid to European refugees from Nazism. After World War II, the organization turned its attention to the state of Israel, and to helping Jews in distress all over the world. Is arming the same as giving?

John Rosenwald told me about a UJA emergency appeal he remembers from one of the Israeli-Arab wars. "Israel was invaded by Egypt and Golda Meir came to the United States and on a Sunday afternoon they assembled the Jewish community of New York at the Waldorf and she looked at the audience and said, 'My country has been invaded and it's very possible we can be pushed into the sea. If your grand-parents had turned left instead of right you'd be living in my country. Now we need your help. I don't have time for you to go home and think about it. I don't have time for you to consult with your tax advisors. I don't have time for you to leave it in your will. I need it right now.'"

As Rosenwald remembers it, Meir raised $300 million for Israel that day, for military expenses.

I may find Hamas reprehensible and the Israeli cause just, and you may feel the other way around, but these dona-tions seem like something other than charity.

Maimonides, however, was not a peacenik. He con-doned fighting wars in certain circumstances. Yet his inclina-tion was always toward fairness; his support of military action seems reluctant at best. "One should not make war against anyone until first calling out to them for peace," he wrote.

Of course, conquest and charity have always been linked. Remember the Crusades? For centuries chivalric notions of knighthood inspired lofty notions of honor, truthfulness, devotion and charity—ideals accompanied by horrific violence and bloodshed, racism and cruelty.

Just as individuals can have mixed motives when they give and receive, so do institutions and governments. Charity has rarely been pure, I was reminded again by James A. Smith, a medieval scholar who divides his time between the academic and foundation worlds, and who was advising the president of the J. Paul Getty Trust when I talked to him. "From the very beginning, charity and gift giving have always had at least two or three purposes and possibly dozens more," he said. "The purposes began to shift as the nature of wealth changed. When you have money you can do one thing. When you have land or the resources produced by the land or you control a toll or you control some revenue-generation stream you behave differently with your charity. The role that has been defined for the state is another."

The regulation of charity began with the growth of nation states in the Middle Ages, as governments began trying to regulate institutional charity to prevent corruption. Maimonides built his ladder in an age when many people were considering the relationship between humans and God, faith and reason. For Smith, one of the most exciting periods was the sixteenth century, when throughout western Europe there were reforming efforts to make charitable gifts more significant to beneficiaries, to end corruption, to rationalize the relation between private charity and municipal and state functions. These reforms were aimed at making sure that charitable gifts—particularly of property—were managed fairly. So if a wealthy person bequeathed the family home to serve as a hospital or an orphanage, for example, the law would make sure someone was assigned to carry out those wishes responsibly.

"They didn't have a term for it in the sixteenth century," said Smith, "but self-dealing was a pretty good label for what people were trying to prevent."

Smith saw resonance of those sixteenth century reform efforts in the debates leading up to the Tax Reform Act of 1969, which significantly changed the relationship between government and philanthropy. The reform came about because of abuses by wealthy donors and their private foundations, getting tax breaks for charities that looked suspiciously like personal whim, rather than a broad social interest. For the first time, the IRS could actively punish foundations making false charity claims, rather than simply revoke their tax-exempt status. There were rules against self-dealing (sic transit Lorraine Hale), and explicit rules meant to force foundations to spend their assets on charity rather than sitting on them.

On and off over the next thirty years, Congress waffled, allowing tax breaks for charitable foundations between 1984 and 1994, both with specific legislation and surreptitiously, for example as an unheralded provision tacked onto a bill that, among other things, raised the minimum wage.

"Here's what this means," explained Monica Langley in the *Wall Street Journal* in 1998. "Instead of giving $20 million to, say, the United Way or to an alma mater, wealthy folks can now plow huge chunks of their fortunes into charities of their own creation—over which they exercise almost total control—and still get big deductions on their taxes."

In her story about a brief reincarnation of the private foundation tax break, Langley described a variety of wealthy families who used it to promote pet charities, which included a college scholarship fund, in one case, and an arts foundation in another. She observed that these private charities are often used to hold families together. "Many foundation meetings are often called during the holidays," she wrote, either because that is when the family is together anyway, or as a way to entice the kids to return home.

Surely anything that brings families together has its virtues, but is it charity—more specifically, should it be tax-deductible?

Langley, during her stint on the philanthropy beat at the *Journal,* provided theme and variation on the charitable tax dodge. In one front-page story she explained how Fidelity Investments' Charitable Gift Fund had swiftly grown to more than $1.5 billion in 1998, rivaling big established charities like the American Red Cross and the Salvation Army, by allowing donors to keep their money growing tax-free until they decided to give it away. There was no timetable, not even the donor's lifetime.

"Some Fidelity givers have used this feature to make contributions that may be improper—such as paying off personal pledges to charities or getting full deductions for glitzy galas," wrote Langley. "Other contributions have been used to fund projects like raising lobsters in captivity." She quoted other foundation operators complaining that Fidelity was stealing their thunder, and that Fidelity was merging its commercial and charitable operations.

The *Journal* investigation didn't uncover deliberate fraud. A few of the donors working through Fidelity said they had inadvertently used their grants for prohibited items, like a Boston woman who used her account to pay for tickets to a charity dinner, which it turned out wasn't entirely tax deductible. But Rambamlike questions of ethics and spirituality lie in the subtext of Langley's straightforward and thorough reports on these tax machinations. As a larger group of Americans has grown richer, while a far larger group has grown poorer by comparison, charity has become more and more entwined with commercial considerations. The more people have to give away, the more concerned they become with maximizing their gifts. Sometimes it seems as if the strategy overwhelms the endgame, which is intended to redistribute some of the wealth. Moving the money around becomes far more time-consuming and interesting than worrying about the inequity that allows us this indulgence.

On my bulletin board hangs a *New Yorker* cartoon in which a prosperous looking man with a briefcase, mouth set grimly, is ignoring a stubble-faced fellow holding out his hat. The man asking for the handout looks annoyed. "It's not as if I'm asking you to acknowledge our common humanity," he says.

Melissa Berman's job is to help very wealthy people negotiate the ladder of charity in a purposeful, financially savvy way that also makes room for the acknowledgement of common humanity. She dismisses the notion that this strategic-planning approach is itself a corruption of the charitable transaction. "Even though these decisions may also have an emotional and spiritual component to them doesn't mean you need to do them communing with yourself alone in a darkened room," she told me. Berman is a small, brisk woman whose practical inclination and brisk style is informed by a restless intellect. It's easy to believe her college major was Old Norse, something interesting and obscure. She is the director of Rockefeller Philanthropy Advisors, a nonprofit organization established by the Rockefeller family in the spring of 2002 to help promote their philosophy. The stated mission: "To help donors create thoughtful, effective philanthropy throughout the world." An ancillary hope was that these educated donors would support pet projects of the Rockefellers.

For Berman, the road to spirituality traverses a nine-step program (life apparently has become more complicated since Rambam built his eight-rung ladder). "Thought is different than motive," she explained. "The thought part is the purely intellectual process that we would love to see more of, which is, 'I have these resources. What is the best way for me to use them?' You can be motivated by a legitimate philanthropic ethical impulse and your giving can still be scattershot and emotional."

Her professional advice is aimed at people with a great deal of money to give away. Much of it could be useful, however, to anyone picking and choosing from that stack of solicitations on the kitchen counter, or juggling the annual school auction, the charity drive at church or temple, the park community cleanup, and the countless other opportunities or demands to volunteer.

"Buying a house is an extremely personal and emotional decision but that doesn't mean you don't want to get an engineer's report," she said, "or that you don't want to have some kind of baseline information about the school system, the community, and the value of the house."

Like Rambam, Berman believes in the power of rules, and her nine-step program is central to her pitch to wealthy clients, addressing their desire for a practical resolution of spiritual concerns. "You're perfectly comfortable giving to your church to help start a soup kitchen," she said. "You have trust that the people there are gong to make their best effort and if it doesn't work it'll be due to a series of things that are understandable. It's when they start to expand their giving that people start losing a sense of comfort."

She urges people to treat giving as they would investing or buying a house: Do research, think about what you're trying to accomplish, understand how much time and money you want to devote. Above all, she said, learn about the middlemen: will they deliver on their promises?

"The issue of trust is often the thing," said Berman. "There's a pervasive sense of discomfort many people feel. That's an enormous barrier to a huge number of people. Can you trust the money you give away is going to be well used?"

To give to someone
you don't know, and to
do so anonymously.

Rambam's life was far from secluded. After years of traveling, his family eventually settled in Fustat, about two miles outside of Cairo. Maimonides became the leader of the local Jewish community; he was also personal physician to the Egyptian sultan and his family. The hectic pace of his life, his inability to accomplish all he wanted to do, feels very familiar. Far from having all the answers, the wise man was hard pressed to manage his schedule. He must have understood how easy it is for the struggle for righteousness to get swamped by everyday demands.

His weariness is evident in a letter he wrote to a young scholar who had been working on a translation of *The Guide of the Perplexed*. "The Lord knows how I have written so much," he complained to Samuel ibn Tibbon, his disciple, who wanted to visit the great man. "I run away from people, hiding where they would not notice me, sometimes I lean against a wall, sometimes I lie down to write because my extreme weakness is conspiring with my age."

129

Then, explaining why their time together will be limited, he writes:

"I live in Fustat, and the Sultan resides in Cairo, and between the two places there are two Sabbath zones. The Sultan has a difficult habit—it is impossible for me to avoid seeing him every morning. If he is weak, or if any of his sons or concubines is sick—I cannot leave Cairo, and I spend most of the day in the Sultan's house. It is impossible to avoid seeing his ministers every day, or an official or two may be sick, and I have to take care of their healing. Therefore—every day I go to Cairo at dawn, and if no trouble or anything new happened, I go back to Fustat after at least half a day. When I arrive, quite hungry, I find the parlor full of non-Jews, important and unimportant, and judges, and officials, a mixed company; they know when I am expected. I dismount from my beast, wash my hands, and go out to apologize for keeping them waiting a few minutes while I eat a quick meal, often the only meal during the day. Then I go to take care of them, and write their prescriptions, and there is coming and going until late at night, and sometimes—may the Torah be my witness—I may be up until two o'clock in the morning. I talk to them lying down from exhaustion, and when the evening is over I can no longer talk. The result is that no man of Israel can speak to me or spend some time with me except on Saturday. They all come after prayer, I guide the community as to what they should do during the week, we have a short reading until noon, and then they leave. Many come back in the afternoon for another reading until the evening prayer.

"This is the way my affairs go, and I only told you a little of what you will see with the help of the Lord, blessed be his name. When you complete the translation you have started . . . come for a visit, not for study, because my time is so limited."

In the context of this busy and public life, anonymity may have become both a practical and a spiritual virtue. While much of his intellectual energy was consumed by philosophical abstraction, Rambam was no aloof scholar, contemplating the world from the safe seclusion of library or temple. Yet his involvement took a heavy toll. The grief that overwhelmed him after his brother's death left him frail and prematurely old, but far from undone. Over the next thirty years he would become court physician to the Egyptian sultan and write significant medical and philosophic texts. He was under constant demand for advice and cure. All of this must have heightened the lure of goodness dispensed from behind a cloak.

He was no selfless saint. Look at how he complains about the responsibilities that earned him a privileged position among his own people and those who held power over them. Somebody else could have taken care of the sultan and his wives, but it's understandable that a man like Rambam, having spent so much of his life in fear or in hiding, would want security for himself and for his family. A certain ambition lay behind his relationship with God, which wasn't kept private but was carried on publicly, through writing and debate.

On the spiritual side, for Maimonides, who lived in relatively small communities, anonymity provided a shield to protect the poor from condescension or feeling obligation. Similarly, Aristotle had urged giving without expectation of anything in return; Rambam's contemporary, St. Francis of Assisi, discouraged public recognition of charitable actions. Today, philanthropists, not-so-rich givers as well, often operate secretly to protect themselves from further solicitation, or to hide from family members and friends who may not approve of the organization they are supporting.

Anonymity may be a more exalted form of charity, but doesn't it depersonalize the process? In today's world, it is so easy to become removed from simple human contact. We shop via the Internet; spend far more time plopped in front of television sets or computer screens than mingling at theaters; conduct our giving by mail. Anonymity is far easier achieved than the awareness that is so crucial to Rambam's philosophy.

Paul Schervish, a sociology professor and director of the Social Welfare Research Institute at Boston College, has spent years studying why people give. Between 1995 and 1997, he and John J. Havens, a senior research associate at his institute, conducted a study of what they called "the caring behavior" of forty-four people in the Boston area. (Like charity, research is rarely pure: the project was financed by a couple of large foundations.) They asked the participants to give weekly reports by telephone on "*all the ways*, formal and informal, they gave material or emotional assistance to others."

The formal giving trends were unsurprising. Almost 90 percent of their sample populations contributed to religious organizations. Those who gave to other causes tended to give much larger sums to organizations that had benefited them or someone close to them.

What most interested the researchers were donations beyond financial contributions to organized charitable causes. These included giving help to family and friends, donating blood and participating in bike-a-thons; volunteering at church bingo parties or after-school sports; taking care of a neighbor's plants or pets or fixing their gadgets. This expanded notion of giving also included emotional support offered to parents, grandchildren, and friends.

Using these widened parameters for giving, here's what they found: "Participants contributed an average of $9,269, or approximately 10 percent of pretax family income in money and goods and 102 person-days per participant in time to provide this care to others both formally, according to traditional definitions of giving and volunteering, and informally, according to our broader definition of voluntary assistance. In addition, they extended an average of 11 loans per participant to other individuals and praised, congratulated or similarly encouraged other people, on average, more than 460 times per participant during the course of the year."

This apparent abundance of generosity was much diminished when the researchers looked solely at contributions to organized charity: only 2.2 percent of family income and 15 person-days of time.

Schervish and Havens took the results of their diary study to postulate an optimistic new theory of social relationships they call "moral citizenship." At a time when other social scientists were deploring the decline in American political engagement, pointing to the decrease in voting, the Boston College team concluded that "far from being a negligent society, America is an intensely caring commonwealth."

They argued that most researchers think about charitable behavior too narrowly, in terms of selflessness and noblesse oblige on the altruistic side, or in terms of guilt and reciprocity on the side of self-interest. They proposed an alternative idea: "Caring behavior is motivated by identification with the needs of others."

These academics may sound like hopeless Pollyannas, ivory tower dreamers, talking in this woozy way about a country still infatuated with guns, where prisons are overloaded and the medical system is breathtakingly unfair. But it's also a huge open place that accommodates fragmented desires, where citizens try to reconcile idealism and realism, to rationalize the apparent incompatibility of freewheeling capitalism with concern for others. Just as we simultaneously are unguarded and suspicious, pornographic and prudish, so are we Americans generous and selfish. No matter where each of us falls on the continuum, we can't afford to ignore one another.

Schervish and Havens's idea of identification struck home with me, because at least once a week I am disgusted by some outrageous act of noncompliance in the social pact. These grievances can be small but loom large in my catalog of selfish behavior. For example, riding home on a crowded subway with my children one day, I watched as an elderly couple entered the train. They didn't appear to be all that hardy.

I was standing next to three seated men, two of them youngish and prosperous looking and in apparent good health. They were white, and I mention this for a reason. The third man was middle-aged, black, and had a cane resting at his feet. His coat was shabby.

They all glanced at the old people and then ignored them. I asked the two healthy-looking men if they'd like to give their seats to the couple. The man was lurching unsteadily. As the young men sat there, looking at me with expressions of utter bafflement, the black man with the cane struggled to his feet and gave up his seat.

"Not you," I said. "I meant them," and pointed at the other two.

Finally, blinking their eyes with the perplexed uncertainty of freshly awakened children, they got up and offered their seats.

My twelve-year-old daughter was about to chastise me for embarrassing her in public (again), when a gentle-looking blonde woman called out, "Bravo." She was sitting nearby with her little girl asleep on her lap, and had been watching this little drama unfold. "It always amazes me when they do that," she said in a low voice, nodding toward the young men, now on their feet. "Refuse to see."

I told her my memories of being visibly pregnant, standing in the subway, scanning the seated passengers and making bets on who would offer a seat. Almost always, it played like this, in descending order: Women with children; women without children; old men; Hispanic men; African American men; young or middle-aged white men. The most privileged were the most insular.

She nodded, remembering her own experiences. We parted with friendly nods and, for me, a new awareness of what recognition can consist of. I felt this was one of those little transformations Marnie Pillsbury had been talking about.

The moment lasted long after the subway doors closed behind me. The woman's succinct evaluation stayed with me:

"Refuse to see."

I thought about the men who refused to see again as I read the advice Schervish and Havens offered to the foundations looking to their research for guidance. "The scolding model of fundraising which seeks to elicit giving and volunteering by bullying, by instilling guilt, and by admonishment, should be replaced by one that engages the individual and seeks to build on the individual's prior experiences of the giving and receiving care and the identification with the fate of another, which are endemic to human love."

These sentiments feel logical and true, and consistent with the noblest aspects of gift-giving, as well with basic emotional truths. Yes, look one another in the eye. See what's troubling someone else.

So what's the attraction of secrecy, which takes away the emotional factor and the attendant warm feelings? Why is anonymity a higher level? Why was it so important to Rambam?

For Maimonides, following Mosaic law and Jewish tradition, the answer was simple. Anonymity was the most foolproof way to protect the pact with God. The giving goes beyond human relationships, avoids hurt feelings, and eliminates praise. In ancient times, achieving righteousness was the goal of alms-giving—not a tax deduction (there was none), not personal aggrandizement or psychological well-being, not even identification with the fate of another.

Righteousness would be its own reward.

There's another kind of anonymity, a different kind of self-protection. One of the members of the Bowery Residents Committee board told me she agonizes over asking friends to contribute to the agency.

"You shouldn't feel bad about asking," I assured her. "It's a good cause."

"I know that," she said. "But when people I know who can afford it don't give anything I can't believe how selfish they are. I'd rather not know."

So, is it unseemly to have the Rockefeller name splashed across the city of New York? Or is it a valuable reminder that great wealth spawns great responsibility—and a particular kind of relationship between rich and poor? If that is the case, why do certain kinds of photo-op philanthropy seem so tacky? One that stuck in my craw was when New York's billionaire mayor Michael Bloomberg purchased a $600 bike to encourage citizens to follow suit in case of a transit strike and then, when a contract was negotiated, gave the bike to an African American boy in Brooklyn. Yes, it was heartwarming to think about this fairytale moment in the life of a boy who suffered from diabetes. And Bloomberg is known to be generous with his wealth, so it wasn't as if this was an uncharacteristic gesture. Yet the nakedness of the political opportunism sullied the gift—for me, that is; probably not for the boy who received it. His delight, at least as reported in

The New York Times, seemed genuine and indisputable.

The mayor was simply following a long tradition. In 1990 James A. Smith, the medieval scholar, and a colleague, investigated the subject of anonymity for a foundation that was considering whether to conceal its identity. They wrote a paper, which—perhaps appropriately, given the subject— was never published but found its way into the archives at Boston College. In a discussion of what they call "the public virtue of charity," they describe the story of Count Thibaut of Champagne, who was well known for his generosity.

"On one occasion he loaded his pack horse with shoes and soothing ointments, intending to give them to the poor as he traveled through the countryside. A monk asked him why he was doing this himself rather than relying on one or another of his many servants to distribute the gifts. Thibaut replied, 'I engender in myself greater love for the poor; I excite among them greater devotion and gratitude so that they will pray for me more frequently and fervently; and I implant a more vivid impression in their hearts.'"

The wish for anonymity, like giving, springs from many motives and fulfills many purposes. It isn't that easy to uncover those motives, however, because most anonymous givers are quite serious about their desire not to be known, as I learned when I tried to find an anonymous donor to interview for this inquiry. Finally, through a friend, after assurances that I had no intention of exposing her identity, I made contact with a woman who was willing to talk about why anonymity was so important to her. Even arrangements for our interview were clandestine: I sent her my phone number through an intermediary, and then she called me.

The woman was thoughtful but prickly. In her middle fifties, she descends from enormous wealth but has tried very hard to forge an identity apart from her family's money. She is a psychotherapist who has spent most of her career counseling and obtaining services for poor people, with a special focus on children and their families, sometimes one-on-one, sometimes through schools and community centers. Her colleagues at work have no idea of her background.

For years she lived this dual existence, so intent on keeping the parts separate that she didn't consider the potential good she could do with her wealth. She certainly wasn't oblivious to the needy; on the contrary, she had devoted her professional life to them. Difficult to grasp as it might seem, she found her family fortune to be a burden, something that set her apart. Even so, she hasn't chosen to live in poverty or even as a middle-class person. She has inhabited the world of privilege to which she was born.

"I certainly benefit from the money that I have," she told me. "I live extremely well. Is it too much of a contradiction to live the way I live and work where I work? Maybe. But that's what I do."

She hinted at bitterness that might help explain her attitudes. Her father was not an heir to a great fortune, but became a wealthy man on his own. When he died, he ultimately left all his money to national parks, and nothing to his children, even though his daughter couldn't recollect his having any particular interest in national parks during his life. "I didn't need or want his money but it was a very interesting decision," said his daughter. "He just wanted to cut us off in every way."

Not until middle age, when she was forty-three, did it occur to her to give away much money—and only then because her mother forced her to do so posthumously. In her will the mother passed along the family money to her four children with the requirement that they disperse it charitably. Unlike the daughter, the mother had always regarded noblesse oblige as something natural. Her philanthropic and social lives were comfortably enmeshed. She tended to support the causes that enhanced traditional notions of enlightenment and beauty, such as botanical gardens and philharmonic orchestras. But her example was unaccompanied by guidance about making charitable decisions.

Three of her children apparently had no problem using their share to openly pursue their individual interests: medicine, environment, and the arts. The fourth child, the anonymous donor who spoke to me, found this obligation troubling, even traumatic, even though she felt passionately about social services and could have seen all kinds of possible uses for the money.

"I just didn't want any part of it," she said. "I never saw myself as a philanthropist or wanting to be known as that." But having been forced into the role by her mother's bequest, the woman hired someone she trusted to help her figure out how to donate the money to causes she believed in. They set up a foundation that would distribute $1 million a year to various organizations that focused on child welfare.

Her immediate desire for anonymity was self-protection: she didn't want to lose the professional independence she continues to work so hard to maintain. But as she learned more about the complications of the foundation world, her anonymity also became pragmatic. It allowed her to evaluate institutions she might give money to as a health-care professional, not as a foundation person. Concern about making the recipients feel shame was incidental. "If you're a philanthropist, people suck up to you," she said. "Why should they be put in that position and why should I?"

She has let her husband—who isn't from a wealthy background—teach her children about money because he is much more comfortable with it. Her twenty-three-year-old son recently began giving money away, and he didn't do it anonymously. "He felt really good about it," said his mother. "I thought he did a great job." She saw virtue in her son's ability to abandon anonymity, a corollary to his ability to fully assume the responsibility of giving.

This story, like much of our thinking about charity, like

Rambam's demands for anonymity, assumes that giving always flows downward, from richer to poorer. What happens when you turn the assumption upside down, and the dispossessed become the givers?

Ronald Williams learned long ago not to make easy assumptions. Williams is program director for the Adult Day Health Care Program, which operates the crisis center for the Bowery Residents Committee. The BRC offers services to homeless people, many of whom are mentally ill, many of whom rely heavily on drugs and alcohol. On a regular day at the crisis center some people are in detox programs, others are deciding whether they want treatment, others are moving from detox into other BRC programs. Some people just drop in for a shower and a safe bed for the night.

Early morning is an especially busy time, when people are being admitted and discharged. For some reason, Tuesday mornings are especially busy and September 11, 2001, was a Tuesday morning. Williams was in his office on Lafayette Street that morning. The crisis center is just below Houston Street, a mile north of New York's downtown financial district. When one of his homeless clients came running up from Prince Street where he usually hangs out, a couple of blocks from the crisis center, he tapped on the window and said, "Mr. Williams, I think something is wrong."

Williams had a special relationship with this client, who'd been his first when he came to the BRC fourteen years earlier as a nurse with plans to stay a few months. The man had told Williams something that had become his guiding principle: "If you let a drunk come into your unit for one night you've saved his life." Williams felt fondly toward this man, now in his late fifties, mentally ill and often disoriented.

But that morning the program director sensed that extra fear and confusion were in the mix. Something was terribly wrong. He brought the man inside to the main room where the television was on. "There's a news flash," one of the clients said. Listening but not comprehending, staff and clients froze into silence.

Williams is a powerful-looking African American man in his fifties, with a graying beard and the hard-won experience to match, beginning with a segregated upbringing in Tulsa, Oklahoma, and including a tour of duty in Vietnam, where he was a medic.

"It reminded me of Vietnam, right before an offensive, when everyone is pensive," Williams told me. "You don't even know what's going to happen, what's going to transpire, but you know something is going to happen and it's going to be dramatic."

Soon enough the streets began to fill with groups of people coming up from lower Manhattan, walking fast. The first group looked as normal as terrified people can look. The next batch was covered in debris, and some, also in blood.

What followed surprised Williams, who thought he was

beyond surprise. "My clients, people who were homeless, people at the lower end of society, were making suggestions to the staff. We put chairs outside, we had a hose attached to a faucet, a nurse came out with what first aid we could muster. When people started coming by covered in stuff we hosed them off. A lot of people just wanted to sit down and get a drink of water. My clients were the ones doing this. They were out offering water, offering help. The clients just pitched in as if they were staff. They were sad because of what was going on, but they were glad to be part of something, to be doing something. They were there."

Were the BRC clients responding to brain signals instructing them to help? Are we wired to cooperate? *The New York Times* has reported that we possibly might be. In an article about scientists who studied neural activity, Natalie Angier wrote: "Hard as it may be to believe in these days of infectious greed and sabers unsheathed, scientists have discovered that the small, brave act of cooperating with another person, of choosing trust over cynicism, generosity over selfishness, makes the brain light up with quiet joy."

Lovely thoughts, but for the BRC clients, the ability to perform charity was a short-lived luxury. Unlike Paolo Alavian, who had the wherewithal to continue to give, or John Rosenwald, for whom fund-raising was part and parcel of being a player in the big leagues, the homeless people were more often recipients or supplicants. In the months after

September 11, Williams saw an increase in depression: People who'd been drinking a couple of beers a day began drinking a quart; marijuana smokers tried crack. "There's a general feeling of non-connection, of not being a person involved in the process," said Williams.

The homeless people on Lafayette Street found themselves, through their charity, part of the community that day. Usually ignored or avoided, or recipients of aid, they had been invited, through disruption of the normal order, to participate in the human exchange as equals. They had, momentarily, dropped the anonymity imposed on them by circumstance and been noticed, for their good work. One woman they helped later returned to the center with a tray of cookies she'd baked, not out of pity but in thanks. Gifts had arrived before, but dispensed as charity, not in return for a favor, and that distinction was huge.

Is that what giving can be, then, a way of involving ourselves in the process of being alive—or, borrowing Angier's expression, of making our brains light up with quiet joy?

At the top of the ladder is the gift of self-reliance. To hand someone a gift or a loan, or to enter into a partnership with him, or to find work for him, so that he will never have to beg again.

M aimonides would have approved of John Ford. That thought occurred to me partway through a graduation ceremony at the Bowery Residents Committee. These ceremonies celebrate the accomplishments of clients who have successfully completed various BRC training programs. The graduates can be young, but more often are middle-aged or older, having first matriculated at the school of hard knocks, which is not a cliché to them, but life.

The graduations are almost always emotional events. The clients tell their stories, sad and desperate histories of life on the streets, addiction to drugs or alcohol, time spent in jail. When they arrive at the BRC, they often belong to the category once described as the "undeserving poor." But no one would think they were anything but deserving by the time they graduate, having worked so hard to overcome their problems, and full of plans for self-sufficiency.

The Maimonides-Ford connection struck me during the ceremony for BRC clients who had spent a year in the agency's Horizons program, which prepares formerly home-less people to enter the work world. Some emerge as jani-tors; others have had specialized training in preparing food or working on computers.

John Ford, the charismatic man who runs the Horizons program, spoke that evening. "Spoke" doesn't really describe what Ford does at the meetings. He proclaims, he rumbles, he roars, he holds forth with the passion of a Holy Roller. But he doesn't sermonize. He comes to these events to praise, not to lecture. Tall, slender and handsome, a former professional basketball player, Ford has a rich baritone voice and theatrical delivery. He'd stand out in any room; in this particular universe he's the North Star. Most of the people there had probably heard him tell his stories before, but that seemed only to reinforce their enthusiasm. They cheered as he began to speak with the rolling cadence of a minister in front of his flock.

"The ceremony reminds me of a fisherman who as he was going off to fish came upon a group of beggars and poor peo-ple and they were asking him to give them some of his fish," he said and then paused, expertly, letting momentum build.

A little louder now, Ford continued. "'Give me some of your fish so I can eat today,' they told him."

The men and women in the audience nodded encouragement.

Ford smiled, his appreciation of the response in evidence,

an actor's pleasure mixed in with a social worker's empathy.

He went on. "The fisherman looked at them and said, 'If you come to me and tell me you're hungry and I give you a fish your hunger will be gone for today.'" Again, the deliberate pause.

Then he moved toward the finale, with a crescendo. "Why don't I teach you how to fish so you can eat for a lifetime?"

That was the traditional punch line, but not the conclusion he'd tailored specially for this crowd.

With the moral of the story driven home, Ford thundered his custom-made coda: "And I see before me a roomful of fishermen!"

The place went wild. At that moment, the wisdom of Maimonides (and Horatio Alger and scores of other optimist philosopher-cheerleaders), as interpreted by John Ford, seemed impeccable. What could be more rewarding to both participant and observer than this demonstration of triumph over adversity, this living proof that hard work and determination could vanquish endemic poverty, addiction and bad luck?

Unquestionably these fishermen and -women stood at the receiving end of the ladder's summit. They represented the BRC elite, and deserved applause. But they were a minority within a subset of the extreme down-and-out. Most of the agency's clients would never make it to self-sufficiency, or even halfway. They were too strung out, too mentally impaired, too unambitious. Did that make them unworthy?

Consider the question from the giver's point of view: Is giving a homeless man a blanket tantamount to killing him?

That's more or less what Andrew Apicella believes, though he wouldn't put it quite that bluntly. He runs Project Outreach for the BRC, the program that actively enlists homeless people to leave the street.

Apicella told me, "Giving those blankets, you're enabling people to not be responsible for their basic necessities."

The question came up as we were driving around in the BRC's Project Outreach van with a couple of social workers for the agency. It had been a brutal winter, though the weather that day was comparatively mild, in the mid thirties, still far from comfortable or safe for those living outdoors. Every once in awhile we stopped and tried to convince a homeless person to come back to the agency and try out a detox program. BRC vans cruise twenty-four hours a day. Only about a half dozen people come in off the streets, of the twenty or so the social workers might approach in a day. It's a slow process.

Andrew and Kevin Martin, his boss, told me the story of Arthur Cafiero, a sixty-year-old alcoholic who had lived on the streets of the Upper West Side for more than a decade. "Everybody loved Arthur and that was his downfall," said Martin. "He lived on the steps of a church, and became known in the community. People brought him food and blankets. This kept him just comfortable enough to refuse help that might have saved his life."

I listened guiltily to the parable of Arthur, not confessing that if being a misguided do-gooder was a sin, I was surely a sinner.

It had been a couple of months since I'd seen David, "my" homeless man, looking thinner even through the camouflage padding of his large parka. He had reappeared in front of the corner store, his usual spot when he was in the neighborhood. I was rushing to the copy shop and then to the post office.

But I stopped to say hello, how are you, any luck starting up again with tube socks?

"I went belly up," he reminded me ruefully. "Financial reverses."

Then he told me his boots were killing his feet. I looked down and saw the boots were in bad shape. I remembered the Reeboks in my husband's closet. On more than one occasion he has inexplicably bought shoes that are too small, worn them for a week or two, and then been unable to return them because they'd been used. The Reeboks, the latest such purchase, had been weighing on his conscience.

"What size shoe do you wear?" I asked David, seeing a way to solve two problems.

"Ten"

"Would you like some brand new Reeboks?"

He lit up. I told him to wait in front of the corner store

while I ran over to the copy shop and post office a few blocks away. I'd be back in ten minutes or so, I assured him.

It too me a little longer than I expected at the copy shop, but still just a few minutes. As I turned the corner heading for the post office I saw David coming out of the building.

"I was looking for you" he told me. A policeman had told him to move away from the corner so he had headed toward the post office, knowing that was my destination.

How little I knew of him or his life, the constant dodge.

"Come with me," I said.

As we walked, I realized I didn't want him to come to my home, even though I felt he was trustworthy. I didn't want to subject him to the policeman again either.

"Go meet me at the little park at the corner, by the benches," I told him. "I'll be there in five minutes—really."

He nodded and walked one way while I ran the other. I quickly found the Reeboks in the closet, making sure to check they were size ten. They looked new. I found a nice shopping bag—this seemed important to me, to offer my gift with proper ceremony—and quickly walked around the corner to the little park. When he saw me coming David looked triumphantly toward a man standing near by. "I told that guy over there you were going to get me sneakers and he told me you wouldn't come back," he said.

Handing him the bag I felt genuinely happy, not superior or even particularly charitable, but rather as though I was giving a present to an appreciative friend. He reached over to hug me. Caught off guard, I hugged him back, knowing full well I had solved nothing for him—or for me—yet feeling no regrets either.

How quickly the ladder can turn into a slide. Or had I finally come to accept the paradox that may be part of any act of giving?

I posed this question to John Ford on another occasion, on a visit to his office at the Horizons job training program. As always, he was wearing an elegant suit, with the air of a man who felt comfortable wherever he was. It quickly became clear to me that this shrewd man knew very well the distance between moral purity and practical exigency, just as Rambam did: putting his variation of teaching a man to fish—giving him a loan—at the highest level of giving, but offering theme and variation on righteousness so as not to discourage those trying to climb the ladder.

Forgetting that I had heard him speak at the graduation a week or two earlier, Ford said, "I always use this saying when I give speeches. 'If you come to me, tell me you're hungry and I have fish, I will not give you a fish sandwich, I'll teach you how to fish.' That is my philosophy. It doesn't always work, but that's my philosophy."

I asked Ford if he ever gives money to people on the street.

"I do," he said, without hesitation. "They say, 'Hey, Big Brother, or Hey, Slim, give me something to eat' and I say,

'Okay, let's go.' And I'll go into the store and buy them something. I will not give a guy money but I'll go buy him something in the store. That's what I do."

I pointed out that he was contradicting himself, and he replied that contradiction may be part of the DNA of charity.

"I think about charity: How much does it help? How much does it hurt?" said Ford. "I talk to guys on the street and hear how they expect money, food, or help from white people, meaning the power structure. My question is this— and it's rhetorical—if they didn't get money from these people with power, would they then say, 'Okay, I have to get up now?' How much does it hurt when people come to depend on charity rather than on themselves? That's the question I have and it's a rhetorical question. I'm not sure."

He continued. "Foundations that give us money, they want outcomes," he said. "They want you to say they gave $25,000 and that in turn helped seven people to get jobs. They want to know how many people can you get jobs for. They want outcomes. Not how many people did you feed? How many people did you talk to on the street and maybe get to the hospital?

"We have an outreach team who brings them in. We give them a shower and feed them and they walk out the door. We may or may not see them again. A very small percentage of those people, who may be scratching when they walk in the door because of bugs, who take a shower and want something to eat, it's a small, small percentage that will move through the continuum of care that we have."

As we talked about his life and how his ideas developed, I saw in John Ford's story—as with so many others—the multiple ingredients that develop an individual's sense of duty. Why some people give and others do not becomes a biographical detail of great importance, a significant land-mark in the mapping of character. Just as some people from the same set of parents find it easier to ski or play music than their siblings, some people seem to have an innate sense of justice. For others goodness feels like something learned, and their willingness to endure the lesson depends on circum-stance and will.

Ford is a polished man who likes fine restaurants and ele-gant suits, and who easily moves between high and low, rich and poor, black and white. -How did a man like that decide to devote himself to helping people so opposite in drive and ability from himself?

Ford, who was born in Tennessee in 1945, was one of three sons. He describes his family, which migrated north to Detroit, as a fairly typical working-class African American family of the era. Father was the head of the family; mother ruled. Cleo Ford had tall boys and figured they would go to college on basketball scholarships; sure enough, two of the three got look-sees from the pros. John Ford, the middle child, went all the way—well, almost. He got to the ABA—

the American Basketball Association, the upstart league—
and onto the Indiana Pacers.

The career lasted only three years but the benefits and
obligations were bountiful nevertheless. Ford first got wind of
the idea of charity as a status symbol in the 1970s, when he was
on the party circuit in Detroit. "Everyone was giving parties,"
he said. "The automobile barons had to have a couple of
blacks, a couple of ball players and you'd have a swinging party.
I'd hear them talking about charity and they would brag. Was
it a matter of one-upmanship? I'm not sure. But they would
talk about how much money they gave to so and so.

"I was reading this morning that so-and-so gave because
it did something for him. A lot of people do that," said Ford.
"Is that okay? Well, I'd rather have someone give $100 mil-
lion because it increases his standing in the community than
not give it."

Ford, making nice money but almost nothing compared
with the rich people he knew back in Detroit, felt pressure to
give back to people who had helped raise him up. He used
that expression, "being raised up," several times, bringing to
my mind the image of Rambam's ladder. For him it represented a poor boy just trying to make it to level ground.

The notion of charity in the black community, as Ford
saw it, was complex. "Black folks might look at a person
who's begging and say, 'I didn't get any help and I made it.
You are dragging my image down and therefore you should

get up off your knees, you should pull your hand in and you should make it like I did.' That's a conservative point of view but that's the way a lot of black folks think, I would say, middle-class blacks on down."

I must have looked surprised.

"You can ask any black woman when she goes into a welfare office to deal with people to try to get entitlements," he said. "They'd rather see a white person sitting at that desk than a black person because that black person will look down on them and treat them like they are some type of enemy—like, this person is lazy, they could get up off their asses and do it."

Yet, he said, the black community is also generous. Giving to the church—directly into the collection plate, no tax deduction—is commonplace. "My mother made sure she had money to get through the week and then to give as much as she could to the church. The church would feed people and help take care of the poor, that's true," he said, adding slyly, "and also pay for the minister's Cadillac. But people feel like giving to the church is giving to God, you're paying your way to heaven. Giving to charity, we don't look at it that way."

He didn't move directly from the party circuit in Detroit to the BRC. Life intervened. He taught high school and coached, married and had a daughter, divorced, moved around. New York became his destination by happenstance, someplace he'd enjoyed on the basketball circuit, a good place to start your life over.

But no accident that he ended up at the BRC, if you want to play amateur analyst. Two brothers in the Ford family made successes of themselves, and then there was Butch, the youngest. He was the one who didn't get a look-see from the pros in college like his older brothers, and instead became a truck driver like their father. That would have been fine, he enjoyed the road, but for whatever reasons he became a drug user.

Then, with a stark note of pain, John Ford repeated himself, as though he didn't believe what he had just said. "My younger brother is a drug user."

The deep baritone faded to meekness. "I just went home recently to get him out of a shelter," he said softly, and then his natural sense of drama stirred him. "Yup!" he exclaimed. "To get him out of a shelter!"

"I stood outside of the shelter and I started crying. I said, 'I'm not going in.' I stood there, my brother walked out and I saw the same clients that I work with here and I cried. 'That is my baby brother coming out of a shelter.'"

More than most people, he understood directly how long a journey it could be from the lowest level to the highest.

As for my journey, I realized it might take forever. After all, Maimonides never stopped grappling with these issues, up until his death at age sixty-nine. But I *had* come to a deeper understanding of Stephen Jay Gould's "great asymmetry." I now agreed with him when he said, "Complex systems can only be built step by step, whereas destruction requires but an instant." Still, I was a little disappointed that I hadn't had an epiphany, the great neon flash of insight that clarified everything. Rambam's Ladder was far more subtle and complicated—like goodness itself.

One day, though, while I was watching a movie on a subject that might seem far removed from this one, I realized that I did understand what Rambam's Ladder has come to mean to me. The movie, a documentary about one of Hitler's secretaries, was called *Blind Spot,* and consisted almost entirely of excerpts from interviews with Frau Traudl Junge, conducted fifty-five years after Hitler's death.

As this elderly and articulate woman revisited her experience in the heart of darkness she didn't seem to be asking for expiation or exoneration, although maybe that was her desire as she confronted her complicity and perplexity: How could she have been in the belly of the beast but seen only Hitler's small kindnesses to her? How had she managed to remain oblivious to the evil taking place all around? Inconsistent as good might be, she implied, evil may be even more paradoxical, more inexplicable. Frau Junge discussed how Hitler created an alternative vision of morality, whose centerpiece was this: "He convinced the German people they had a task to do. They had to exterminate the Jews, because the Jews caused all our problems," she explained. "It wasn't Hitler's own idea. It had been put forth much earlier, that they had to make a sacrifice."

She recalls reading an interview with a soldier who had been stationed at a concentration camp. The journalist asked the guard, "Didn't you feel any pity at all for the people you treated so badly there?"

"And he replied, 'Yes, I certainly did feel pity for them but I had to overcome it. That was a sacrifice I had to make for the greater cause.'"

As Frau Junge saw it, "That's what happened to conscience. After all, Hitler always used to say: You don't have to worry, any of you. You just have to do whatever I say and I'll take responsibility. As if anyone can take charge of another person's conscience. I do think you can make someone's conscience more sensitive or desensitize it or manipulate it."

The secretary's words chilled me, but also made me wonder: If Frau Junge was correct, and history has proved over and over that she might be, could her theory be applied for good? Was it possible to make conscientiousness a national imperative, to make awareness and empathy the dutiful sacrifice for the greater cause?

Probably not. If I'd learned anything from my excursion up and down Rambam's Ladder, it was that empathy couldn't be mandated, and that charity shouldn't be thought of as a sacrifice. Goodness can't be willed into being.

But it can be instilled—not by forcing employees to give, or by promising children better grades if they do good deeds, or by spending too much time analyzing whether the tithe should be taken before or after taxes. But simply by opening your eyes, by paying attention, by not letting those "spectacular incidents of evil," as Gould called them, eclipse the less dramatic but profound acts of goodness that take place every day.

Recalling the World Trade Center attacks again, I remembered the reaction of our local elementary school, where many children had witnessed the destruction from their classroom windows. Within months, after the United States retaliated against the terrorists by bombing Afghanistan, the school organized a dance to raise money for an Afghan school. For my son, this wasn't an act of charity, but a logical transfer from richer to poorer that made far more sense to him than the violence that had upended his world.

The hopefulness of those elementary school children is echoed for me on every rung of Rambam's Ladder. We can't anticipate evil, or forestall ordinary difficulty and grief. But we do have a choice in our response to what life throws at us. Maimonides could have survived by meekly succumbing to the people who hated him simply for who he was. He could have spent his days plotting revenge. Instead, he devoted his life to convincing people that they had it in them to do better than those who had come before. Step by step, rung by rung, all of us can improve ourselves—and the world.

That, for me, is the highest level of giving, an antidote to the rhetoric of righteousness invoked so often and fruitlessly to legitimize war and destruction. Giving SHOULD NOT BE an afterthought; what nations do to repair the damage they've inflicted on one another, what individuals do to assuage their guilt for their excesses or indifference. But the building material for every step of Rambam's Ladder is conscientiousness—and consciousness. Anonymity, self-sufficiency, absence of reluctance, not inflicting shame: all of these ideas mandate an awareness of our common humanity. They remind us that in the end we are not measured by what we have, but by what we give to one another.

NOTES

INTRODUCTION

Page 00:

Stephen Jay Gould, "A Time of Gifts," *The New York Times,* September 26, 2001.

Page 00.

Biographical details of Maimonides' life are well documented in Ilil Arbel, *Maimonides: A Spiritual Biography* (New York: Crossroad, 2001) and Abraham Joshua Heschel, *Maimonides: A Biography* (New York: Farrar, Strauss, Giroux, 1982).

Page 00.

See "Treatise II: Gifts to the Poor" in Moses Maimonides, *The Code of Maimonides, Book 7: The Book of Agriculture,* trans. Isaac Klein, Yale Judaica Series (New Haven: Yale University Press, 1979), 91–93.

Page 00.

Contributions to major organizations: The Center on Philanthropy at Indiana University, *Giving USA 2002,* (Indianapolis: AAFRC Trust for Philanthropy, 2002).

Page 00.

Larry Neumeister, "Ex-Sotheby's Chairman Gets Year in Prison, $7.5 million Fine," *Boston Globe,* April 22, 2002.

Page 00.

Statistics on foundation giving: See the Web site of the
Foundation Center for updated reports on foundations and giv-
ing: http://fdncenter.org See also: "Foundation Gifts Rose 18% in
2000, New Report Says," *The Chronicle of Philanthropy,* July 26,
2001. Geoffrey Cowley, Tom Masland, and Anne Underwood,
"Bill's Biggest Bet Yet," *Newsweek,* February 4, 2002. Center on
Philanthropy at Indiana University, *Giving USA 2002.* Ronald
Alsop, "Perils of Corporate Philanthropy," *The Wall Street Journal,*
January 16, 2002.

RELUCTANCE
Page 00.

The experiments were reported in *Journal of Personality and Social
Psychology* 79, no.6.

Page 00.

Roger Segelken, "CU Researchers' Study Shows Americans
Aren't as Nice as They Think," *Cornell Chronicle,*
March 29, 2001.

Page 00.

Randy Cohen, "Grading Charity," *The New York Times Magazine,*
April 6, 2003.

Page 00.

Citigroup Annual Report 2002

PROPORTION

Page 00.

Roger Lowenstein, *Buffett: The Making of an American Capitalist*
(New York: Random House, 1995). Mr. Buffett and his wife give
some money away now, but a tiny percentage of what he has.

Page 00.

U.S. adult giving: Center on Philanthropy at Indiana University,
Giving USA 2002.

Page 00.

Ilil Arbel, *Maimonides: A Spiritual Biography*
(New York: Crossroad, 2001), 98.

Page 00.

Stephanie Strom, "Billions in Charity Money Could Be Saved,
Study Says," *The New York Times,* May 10, 2003.

Page 00.

Twentieth-century data: *The New Nonprofit Almanac and Desk
Reference* (San Francisco: Jossey-Bass, 2002).

Page 00.

http://www.forbes.com/home/2002/02/28/billionaires.html

Page 00.

Census statistics are quoted from Robert Pear, "Number of
People Living in Poverty Increases in U.S.," *The New York Times,*
September 25, 2002.

Page 00.

See http://www.oecd.org and http://www.globalissues.org.

Page 00.

Paul Goodman, "The Psychology of Being Powerless," *The New York Review of Books,* November 3, 1966.

Page 00.

"Zoom": Nickelodeon, the cable channel for children owned by Viacom International, Inc., has a similar program, "The Big Help," which encouraged about 40 million children to pledge more than 383 million volunteer hours between 1994 and 2001.

SOLICITATION

Page 00.

Maimonides, *The Code of Maimonides,* trans. Isaac Klein, Yale Judaica Series (New Haven: Yale University Press, 1979).

Page 00.

Gerald Wilkinson, "Food Sharing in Vampire Bats," *Scientific American,* February 1990, 80.

Page 00.

Maimonides quote from "Meditations," Siddur, *Gates of Repentance: The New Union Prayerbook for the Days of Awe,* Chaim Stern, ed. (New York: Central Conference of American Rabbis, 1978).

Page 00.

Ilil Arbel, *Maimonides: A Spiritual Biography*
(New York: Crossroad, 2001).

Page 00.

"Poster boy": Anthony DePalma, "Giving When 'Rosie' Asks,
New York's Elite Can't Say No," *The New York Times,*
November 20, 2000.

Page 00.

Rotary International Web site:
http://www.rotary.org/aboutrotary/history/earlyyears.html.

SHAME

Page 00.

An-Nawawi, *Forty Hadith of an-Nawawi,* trans. Ezzeddin Ibrahim
and Denys Johnson-Davies, (Cambridge, UK: Islamic Texts
Society, 1997).

Page 00.

"Gifts to the Poor": Maimonides, *The Code of Maimonides.*

Page 00.

Gertrude Himmelfarb: Interview in "Learning from Victorian
Virtues," *Religion and Liberty* 5, no. 4. And: Gertrude Himmelfarb,
The Demoralization of Society: From Victorian Virtues to Modern Values
(New York: Knopf, 1995).

Page 00.

Rambam: Chaim Stern, ed., *Gates of Repentance.*

Page 00.

David Brooks, "Why the U.S. Will Always Be Rich," *The New York Times Magazine,* June 9, 2002.

BOUNDARIES
Pages 00–00.
Peter Singer, *Practical Ethics,* 2d ed.
(New York: Cambridge Univerity Press, 1993).

Pages 00–00.

Karen Wright, "Generosity versus Altruism: Philanthropy and Charity in the US and UK," Civil Society Working Paper Series, The Centre for Civil Society (London: London School of Economics, 2002). See also Center on Philanthropy at Indiana University, *Giving USA 2002.*

CORRUPTION
Page 00.
Lorraine Hale, *House that Love Built*
(New York: Hale House, 1991).

Page 00.

Heidi Evans and Dave Saltonstall, "Charity Begins at Home for Hale House; Millions Went to Fund-raising, Not Kids, *New York Daily News,* April 18, 2001. See also Nina Bernstein, "Officials Overlooked Dire Signs at Charity," *The New York Times,* February 7, 2002.

Page 00.

Ben Brantley, "The Early Civil Rights Movement, Set to Music," *The New York Times,* July 22, 1994

Page 00.

Heidi Evans and Dave Saltonstall, "Lorraine Hale's $1.3M Slush Fund; Hidden Cash, Insurance Payoff Are Discovered in Probe," *New York Daily News,* August 8, 2001.

Page 00.

Internet postings: For more information, see GuideStar, the registered trademark and operating name of Philanthropic Research, Inc., a 501(c)(3) nonprofit organization: http://www.guidestar.org

Page 00.

Taubman: See the Cybersurveys archive of the *Detroit News* Web site: http://www.detnews.com.

Page 00.

An article which fully details the Holy Land Foundation situation is Glenn R. Simpson, "Holy Land Foundation Allegedly Mixed Charity Money With Funds for Bombers," *The Wall Street Journal,* February 27, 2002. See also, Neely Tucker, "Muslim Charity's Lawsuit Raises 'Distressing' Issues, Judge Says," *The Washington Post,* April 23, 2002.

Page 00.

Maimonides, *The Code of Maimonides,* trans. Isaac Klein, Yale Judaica Series (New Haven: Yale University Press, 1979).

Page 00.

Monica Langley, "A Tax Break Prompts Millionaires' Mad Dash To Create Foundations," *The Wall Street Journal,* January 27, 1997. And Monica Langley, "You Don't Have to Be a Rockefeller to Set Up Your Own Foundation," *The Wall Street Journal,* February 12, 1998.

ANONYMITY

Page 00.

Ilil Arbel, *Maimonides: A Spiritual Biography* (New York: Crossroad, 2001), 168.

Page 00.

Paul G. Schervish and John J. Havens, "The Boston Area Diary Study and the Moral Citizenship of Care," *Voluntas: International Journal of Voluntary and Nonprofit Organizations* 13, no.1 (March 2002): 47–71.

Page 00.

Clifford J. Levy, "Mayor Donates 'Strike Bike' to an Ailing Boy in Brooklyn," *The New York Times,* December 26, 2002.

Page 00.

Natalie Angier, "Why We're So Nice: We're Wired to Cooperate," *The New York Times,* July 23, 2002.

RESPONSIBILITY

Page 00.

Stephen Jay Gould, "A Time of Gifts," *The New York Times,* September 26, 2001.

BIBLIOGRAPHICAL NOTE

For this inquiry I examined a wide range of different aspects of altruism, including genetics, evolution, animal behavior, ethics, moral psychology, literary fiction, welfare policy, political science, the tax system, voluntarism, philanthropy, poverty around the world, and religion. My sources were academic journals, policy papers, newspapers, magazines, the Internet, advertisements, interviews, and books. Of the many interesting and useful volumes I examined, particularly helpful were Robert H. Bremner, *Giving: Charity and Philanthropy in History* (New Brunswick, N.J.: Transaction, 1994); Richard Dawkins, *The Selfish Gene.* New ed. (New York: Oxford University Press,1989); Garrett Hardin, *The Limits of Altruism: An Ecologist's View of Survival* (Bloomington; Indiana University Press, 1977); Philippa Foot, *Virtues and Vices and Other Essays in Moral Philosophy* (Berkeley: University of California Press, 1978); Robert A. Liston, *The Charity Racket.* 1st ed. (Nashville; University of Tennessee Press, 1977); Heather MacDonald, *The Burden of Bad Ideas: How Modern Intellectuals Misshape our Society* (Chicago: Dee, 2000); Myron Magnet, ed. *What Makes Charity Work? A Century of Public and Private Philanthropy* (Chicago: University of Chicago Press, 2000); James Rachels, *The Elements of Moral Philosophy* (Philadelphia: Temple University Press, 1986); James M. Ratcliffe, *The Good Samaritan and the Law* (Garden City, N.Y.: Anchor, 1966); Peter Singer, *Practical Ethics.* 2d ed. (New York: Cambridge University Press, 1993); Lauren

Wispe, ed. *Altruism, Sympathy and Helping; Psychological and Sociological Principles* (New York: Academic Press, 1978).

There were many texts that proved very useful on the subject of modern philanthropy, but the most interesting for a general reader would be Ron Chernow, *Titan: The Life of John D. Rockefeller, Sr.* (New York: Random House, 1998); Roger Lowenstein, *Buffett: The Making of an American Capitalist* (New York: Random House, 1995). For discussions on the state of modern philanthropy, papers by the Boston College Social Welfare Research Institute were invaluable.

While many books about Maimonides were helpful in the course of my research and writing, three were especially informative: Kenneth Seeskin, *Maimonides: A Guide for Today's Perplexed* (West Orange, N.J.: Behrman, 1991); Abraham Joshua Heschel, *Maimonides: A Biography* (New York: Farrer, Straus, Giroux, 1982); Ilil Arbel, *Maimonides: A Spiritual Biography* (New York: Crossroad, 2001). An important text to note is the original version of Maimonides' Ladder of Charity, translated by Isaac Klein, which is found in Moses Maimonides, *The Code of Maimonides, Book 7: The Book of Agriculture* (New Haven; Yale University Press, 1979). Another work of Maimonides that is worth mentioning is his *The Guide of the Perplexed,* trans. Shlomo Pines (Chicago: University of Chicago Press, 1956). Also of interest are the ideas of other scholars whose work is often mentioned in connection with Maimonidean thought: Averroes, Thomas Aquinas, *Summa Theologiae;* Aristotle, *Nicomachean Ethics, Book 8.*

Julie Salamon

J ulie Salamon, a culture writer for *The New York Times,* was previously a reporter and film critic for *The Wall Street Journal.* Her journalism has also been published in *The New Yorker, Vanity Fair, Vogue,* and *The New Republic.*

Salamon is the author of five previous books: the novel *White Lies; The Devil's Candy,* about the making of *Bonfire of the Vanities* ("As close to a definitive portrait of the madness of big-time movie-making as we're likely to get"— *Newsweek*); *The Net of Dreams* (a family memoir that *Newsday* found "honest, true, deeply touching"); *The New York Times* bestseller *The Christmas Tree,* and, most recently, *Facing the Wind* (which *USA Today* said "elevates itself out of the true crime genre into literature"). *The Christmas Tree* was turned into an ABC-TV movie directed by Sally Field and starring Julie Harris; the book's audio version won the 1997 Audie Award for best inspirational audiobook.

A native of Seaman, Ohio, Julie Salamon is a graduate of Tufts University and New York University Law School. She lives in Manhattan with her husband, Bill Abrams, and their two children, Roxie and Eli.